TRESPASSERS ON THE AMAZON

John Ure

TRESPASSERS
ON THE AMAZON

Constable · London

First published in Great Britain 1986
by Constable and Company Limited
10 Orange Street, London WC2H 7EG
Copyright © John Ure 1986
Set in Linotron Ehrhardt 11 pt by
Rowland Phototypesetting Limited
Bury St Edmunds, Suffolk
Printed in Great Britain by
St Edmundsbury Press Limited
Bury St Edmunds, Suffolk

British Library CIP data
Ure, John
Trespassers on the Amazon
1. Amazon River Watershed – Exploration
– History
I. Title
918.1'104   F2546

ISBN 0 09 466500 1

For

ARABELLA

Henceforth, wherever thou may'st roam
My blessing like a line of light,
Is on the waters day and night,
And like a beacon guards thee home.

CONTENTS

Prologue   11

1   The Pioneers   15
2   The Enquirers   30
3   The Raider   48
4   The Railroad Men   57
5   The Investigators   69
6   The Adventurer   91
7   The Seeker for El Dorado   107
8   The Literary Men   128
9   The Developers   143
10   The Contemporaries   154
Epilogue   165
Bibliography   171
Index   174

ILLUSTRATIONS

Map of the Amazon Basin 21
Map of Fawcett and his followers 110

between pages 32 and 33

Sir Walter Raleigh (*National Portrait Gallery*)
Sir Thomas Roe (*National Portrait Gallery*)
Fortifications at Belém
Alfred Russell Wallace (*BBC Hulton Picture Library*)
H A Wickham (*National Portrait Gallery*)
Carajas Indians on Aragayan River
Travelling under sail off Marajo Island
Abandoned engines of the Madeira-Mamoré railway
Sir Roger Casement (*BBC Hulton Picture Library*)
Theodore Roosevelt in 1910 (*BBC Hulton Picture Library*)

between pages 64 and 65

A warrior of the Xavante tribe
A Xavante warrior
Tribal ceremony of the Xingu tribe
Colonel P H Fawcett (*Royal Geographical Society*)
Rattin, Swiss trapper (*from a private collection*)
A Xingu house in construction and life inside a hut of the Tucano
    tribe
Riverside life at Iquitos
Cattle ranching at Marajo Island
Buffalo on Marajo Island
Alligators in a swamp

between pages 96 and 97

A Xingu mother
A rubber tapper's house
Peter Fleming (*National Portrait Gallery*)
Evelyn Waugh (*National Portrait Gallery*)
Wildlife of the Amazon (*The Zoological Society of London*)
Robin Hanbury-Tenison and Richard Mason (*R Hanbury-Tenison*)
The headwaters of the Amazon
Map of South America, engraved in 1562 (*British Library*)
The author at one of the sources of the Amazon

Except where otherwise stated, all photographs are by Caroline Ure or the author. Maps drawn by Andrew Bell.

ACKNOWLEDGEMENTS

The literature about travel on the Amazon is voluminous. It seems at times that every Anglo-Saxon who has ventured into these parts has felt it incumbent on him to write down, and if possible publish, an account of his experiences. With so much source material available, the author has been particularly indebted to those who have helped him sort the wheat from the chaff: the late Earl of Birkenhead, Dr John Hemming (director of the Royal Geographical Society) and Dr Jose Mindlin (of São Paulo) have been especially kind in this respect.

I am also very grateful to Dr Helen Wallis (Keeper of the Map Room at the British Museum) and to the staffs of the Foreign and Commonwealth Office library and the Royal Geographical Society library who have been to immense trouble to obtain obscure books for me.

But my greatest debt of gratitude is to all those friends in Brazil—both Brazilians and diplomatic colleagues—who, knowing of my interest in Amazonian travel, have directed me towards sources of information: newspaper articles, manuscript letters and reports, and even verbal recollections.

Lastly, I wish to record appreciation of those who have helped me reach the places about which I have been writing. Here special mention must be made of Mr John Shakespeare (HM Ambassador to Peru) and his wife Lalage who took us with them on treks to the headwaters of the Amazon, and also of the Brazilian Air Force—an intrepid force of skilful fliers who have transported us to places we could have reached in no other way. To all these my thanks are due.

PROLOGUE

There are few waterways in the world on which the Anglo-Saxon races have not made themselves at home. Britannia has not only ruled the waves on the world's seas, but has frequently ruled the ripples on the world's rivers too. The Ganges and the St Lawrence have seen British adventurers, soldiers and merchants establishing themselves on their banks. The story of the Nile—both White and Blue—is bound up with the names of Anglo-Saxon explorers like Burton, Livingstone and Stanley, or with Generals like Gordon, Kitchener and Napier—as all readers of Alan Moorehead's famous twin volumes are aware. The Mississippi—particularly since the time of Mark Twain—is an integral part of American folk-lore as well as of American history. The banks of the Danube and the Rhine have rung to the clash of British arms. Even over the desert hinterland of the Tigris and Euphrates, the sound of Anglo-Saxon voices has resounded from archaeological sites, oil rigs and Arab encampments.

Almost alone among the world's great waterways the Amazon has remained remote from the British and Americans. Alien by history as well as by geography, the vast forests enclosing its muddy waters have for centuries been a forbidden as well as forbidding domain. Those Englishmen who first came here found no welcome: earlier European settlers had staked out claims at the river's mouth and felt that this gave them a right to be possessive about the 4000 miles of water that lay up-stream of them. The indigenous inhabitants, though not unfriendly at first, were soon persuaded that Englishmen were dangerously transient patrons. What force of civilization there was, was of a militantly religious nature, actively hostile to protestant heretics. For seventeenth or nineteenth century adventurers—whether from Bristol or Plymouth, from New England or New Orleans—there were equally tantalizing regions elsewhere in the world to explore and in which to settle, where the odds were not so heavily weighted against them.

Nor was the Amazon congenial even to those who claimed it as their own. The heat and humidity debilitated all but the most hardy. The mosquito was for centuries to take its toll of those ignorant of the origins of malaria. The river's banks were as nearly impenetrable as any jungle in the world. The abuse of the Indians quickly had the effect of adding poisoned darts and arrows to the natural hazards of venturing into the unknown. The animal life of the Amazon forests, while possibly less spectacular than that of Africa or India, was equally as lethal: the jaguar's pounce could be as deadly as the lion's, the puma's as the tiger's. And in reptiles—a form of life peculiarly repugnant to most Anglo-Saxons—the Amazon basin seemed to set new standards of revulsion: thirty-foot boa-constrictors to drop on and crush the unwary, bushmasters as aggressive as king-cobras, coral snakes as poisonous as krites, alligators as menacing as any crocodile. Even the stream itself harboured man-eating fish. This seemed an alien world indeed into which to penetrate even without the human hostility which compounded its unwelcome.

And yet, penetrate it the English and later the Americans did. First they came as pioneers attempting to settle; then as naturalists to identify and classify new species; occasionally as raiders to filch the precious rubber seedlings; later as investigators to reveal and denounce barbarities against the Indians; frequently as seekers for El Dorado or simply for adventure; sometimes as literateurs hankering after new environments; often—rifle in hand—as sportsmen; and latterly as developers attempting to swamp the world with Amazonian rubber tyres or wood-pulp. For all of them it was hard and hazardous; for many it was ruinous or fatal.

This book attempts to chronicle the exploits of these rare Anglo-Saxon trespassers in a world which, for four centuries, has both allured and repelled them. Most of their stories have been told elsewhere in different contexts, but occasionally —while living in Brazil as ambassador of the country of origin of many of those about whom I was writing—I have stumbled on new facts and fresh documents. I have also tried to see for myself the conditions which my compatriots and other Anglo-Saxon travellers encountered: I have trekked to the head-waters of the Amazon river-system in the Peruvian Andes, and have visited—often by canoe—mission stations and Indian villages not only on the banks of the main waterways of Amazonas and Pará but also along the creeks and backwaters of Mato Grosso. I offer the results as a tribute to all those Britons and Americans who have shared my fascination with the world's most daunting river.

THE PIONEERS

King Henry VIII of England shared with his remote descendant Queen Victoria a marked propensity to be unamused. But on one autumn day in 1531, at his brand new palace of Whitehall, he was very much amused indeed. He had just been shown a remarkable and most diverting phenomenon which had never been seen in his kingdom before. Sir William Hawkins of Plymouth*, one of his most enterprising merchant seamen, had been displaying to him a feather-decked but otherwise naked Indian chief. The chief had particularly aroused the merriment of King Henry's taffeta and silk clad courtiers on account of the bones stuck through his cheeks and lips, which—it had been explained to them—denoted that he was a man of military prowess in his own country.

That country was a newly discovered land on the fringes of the western ocean. It had previously been piously named by its Portuguese discoverers 'The Land of the True Cross', but subsequently it had become more generally known by the name of the wood that was found there and which provided a lucrative trade on account of the dye produced from it: by 1531 the country was commonly called Brazil.

There was only one slightly worrying aspect of the Brazilian chief's appearance at the English court: a hostage had had to be left behind in that strange and distant land as a guarantee of the chief's safe return. One of Hawkins' fellow citizens of Plymouth—a certain Martin Cockeram—had been abandoned on the coast of Brazil while his captain brought the chief

* The father of the even more celebrated Elizabethan seafarer, Sir John Hawkins.

home for royal and other inspection. And the worry was that the chief found the cold of London—possibly in part due to his scanty attire—far from healthy. In fact, his physical condition had been giving Hawkins anxiety and (had he known of it) would have been giving the unfortunate Cockeram considerably more anxiety.

As soon as he reasonably could, Hawkins re-embarked for the New World taking the ailing chief with him. But it was too late. In mid-ocean the chief succumbed—probably of pneumonia—and died. Cockeram's chances of survival looked slim indeed. But Hawkins shared with many of his West-country compatriots a trust-worthy manner and a reputation for straight dealing with men of all conditions—be they over-dressed courtiers or under-dressed tribesmen. The Brazilian Indians who had lent him their chief accepted that he had taken all proper care of their leader and that the latter's unfortunate demise did not indicate foul play or bad faith. They handed back a somewhat under-nourished Cockeram and allowed Hawkins to sail away in search of other merchandise. The first contact between the natives of the Amazon delta and the peoples of the Anglo-Saxon world had passed off, if not successfully, at least less badly than might have been.

But the contact was not kept up. Hawkins and his fellow Tudor seafarers concentrated their attentions much further north—on the Spanish Main and among the islands of the West Indies. Little was heard in Plymouth, or Bristol, let alone in London or Greenwich, of the vast forests further south, until towards the end of the sixteenth century.

There were occasional English mariners who reached South America. The most remarkable of these was Anthony Knivet —also from Plymouth—who spent the best part of a decade (1591–1601) having adventures up and down the Brazilian coast. Sometimes he was trading in Indian slaves; sometimes he was himself a slave of the Portuguese; sometimes he was living with cannibal tribes in the forests. He had the most remarkable capacity for survival and wrote a graphic account of his exploits, which reveal him as the first Englishman to experience many of the hazards of the region. He recounts how 'a great thing came out of the water, with great scales on the backe, with great ugly clawes and a long tayle . . .' which seems certain to have been an early encounter with an alligator. But Knivet, although he explored the coast both north and south of Rio de Janeiro, does not appear to have penetrated the Amazon nor its great sister river and neighbour to the north—the Orinoco. This was left to the most celebrated of all Elizabethan adventurers, Sir Walter Raleigh, whose expedition up the Orinoco in 1595 was to be the direct inspiration of immediately subsequent English expeditions up the Amazon.

Raleigh's famous voyage 500 miles up the Orinoco was a disappointment to his sponsors, such as Queen Elizabeth, and to his financial backers, such as the Queen's counsellor Cecil: Raleigh had not found the fabled El Dorado and had brought back little gold or precious stones. But he had brought back vivid impressions of a rich jungle land 'that hath yet her maidenhood'; his description of the terrain of 'the Large, Rich and Bewtiful Empire of Guiana' could equally be taken as a description of the even less known terrain of the Amazon. His accounts of 'the common delights of hunting, hawking, fishing, fowling' were taken to embrace all the rain forests of the region; his conviction that here in this jungle continent was to be found the golden city, in which both Spaniards and Indians believed, was infectious.

Raleigh was to make a later, fatal voyage up the Orinoco in 1617 having been released from the Tower by King James I in the renewed expectation of his bringing back riches. However tragic the personal outcome of that voyage was to Raleigh— and he lost his son on the Orinoco, and his own life was forfeited on his return—it did not disabuse him of his belief that the jungles of South America were a land, if not of milk and honey then at least of gold and game. The seeds of curiosity and cupidity were effectively sewn among his fellow countrymen.

[17]

Indeed, no other Elizabethan could have kindled interest and aroused imaginative speculation as effectively as Sir Walter Raleigh, for Raleigh was the greatest self-publicist in an age not lacking in such talents. He it was who had arrived in London 'a bare gentleman' and had so dazzled the Queen with his manners that she had chosen him as captain of her personal bodyguard; he it was who wore pearls so loosely sewn to his cloak that they scattered around him as he strode through the London streets—a casual benefaction to the gaping citizenry; he it was of whom his jealous judges said 'You have lived like a Star at whom the World hath Gazed'. It was little wonder that this raciest of Elizabethans had managed to put South America including Brazil on the Englishman's map in a manner which no one before him had achieved, and which was to inspire lesser adventurers for the immediately following half century.

Among the first of his followers was Sir Thomas Roe who in February 1610 (seven years before Raleigh's own last exploit) sailed from Dartmouth with two ships, partly financed by Raleigh, to the mouth of the Amazon which he reached at the end of April. Following Raleigh's precedent in the Orinoco, he proceeded to sail his ships boldly up-river for 200 miles, and then—probably at the confluence of the Amazon and the Tapajos—transferred his crew into the ships' boats and proceeded upstream for a further 100 miles.

Like Raleigh, Roe was entranced by what he saw. Although the Indians were not able to provide him with very adequate food supplies, he and his companions 'entred the Country by Indian Boates, and went over the Chatoracts and hills . . . with great labour and perill', eventually linking the northern tributaries of the Amazon with the southern tributaries of Raleigh's Orinoco. The whole trip took thirteen months, not counting the atlantic crossings. Again, the expected gold and gems had not been forthcoming; but again also, the expectations from the region remained undimmed. Indeed, Roe reported in a letter to Cecil that having 'seen more of this coast, rivers and inland

[18]

from the Great River of the Amazones ... than any other Englishman now alive' he was convinced that the region 'hath much wealth upon yt'.

Roe took a further significant action on the Amazon: he left twenty men behind to form a trading station. They constituted one of the first European settlements on the river, as it was a further five years before the Portuguese founded Belém do Pará on the branch of the Amazon's delta closest to the Atlantic. Roe himself did not return but was appointed ambassador to the Great Mogul at Agra in India; while there he received news from his friend Lord Carew that:

'some foure or fyve of your men, lefte in the River of Amazons, are richelye retourned in a Holland shippe. The rest of your men remayne there; those which are come home are ryche, and (as I heare) they meane to retourne. Itt is sayed, that these five brought with them muche Tobacco ... and allso itt is reported that they brought home ingotts of gold, but of what valew I know nott.'

Settlement and trade of a sort had clearly begun.

The reference to 'a Holland shippe' is significant. In fact, the Dutch joined with the English in the early years of the seventeenth century in establishing a number of trading settlements on the Amazon. Another nearly contemporary account* reports that when a ship returned from the Amazon to Flushing in 1623, nine Englishmen promptly trans-shipped to London where they reported favourably on trading conditions and 'how few (of their number) they had buryed in six years'. These reports 'put divers people upon the wing from London' to the Amazon—though some seem to have perished at sea before they even reached the estuary of their destination.

By now there was a move in London to institutionalize the hitherto haphazard trade along the lower reaches of the

* Colonel John Scott's *History & Description of the River of the Amazons* (1660).

Amazon. Captain Roger North, who had been one of Raleigh's officers on his 1617 expedition, approached the Privy Council and eventually got a Commission of Discovery authorizing him to set up an Amazon company to trade, with certain privileges and immunities, up that river. Prominent and wealthy noblemen put up money for the company, including the Earls of Arundel, Rutland, Warwick and Dorset.

But there was one implacable opponent of this new venture, in the person of Count Gondomar—the Spanish Ambassador to the English court. Gondomar was a highly effective diplomat. He had established a strong ascendency over King James I, based partly on threats and partly on flattery. The threats were of retribution by the united force of Spain and Portugal (the latter kingdom having been absorbed—temporarily as it turned out—into the former in 1580), and his nerve was strong enough to threaten his own recall to Madrid—as a prelude to such retribution—if he did not get his own way with the King. The flattery was more subtle: Gondomar boasted in his correspondence with Spain that he pretended to be the King's pupil both in statecraft and in scholarship; James's susceptibility to compliments on his command of Latin and of the cadences of English prose was well known. The King not only showered Gondomar with costly presents—a form of attention he normally reserved for his favourites – but he had in the past gone so far as to leak to Gondomar the details of Raleigh's plans and dispositions for his final Orinoco expedition.

Gondomar had first shown his muscle on Raleigh's return from his last Orinoco expedition: on that occasion he had orchestrated the clamour for Raleigh's execution (at one stage even obtaining King James's promise that Raleigh would be handed over to him for public hanging in Madrid). Now he was preparing to flex his muscles again.

Count Gondomar saw the Amazon company as a direct menace to Spanish/Portuguese dominion, and he was determined to frustrate its purposes. To this end he persuaded King

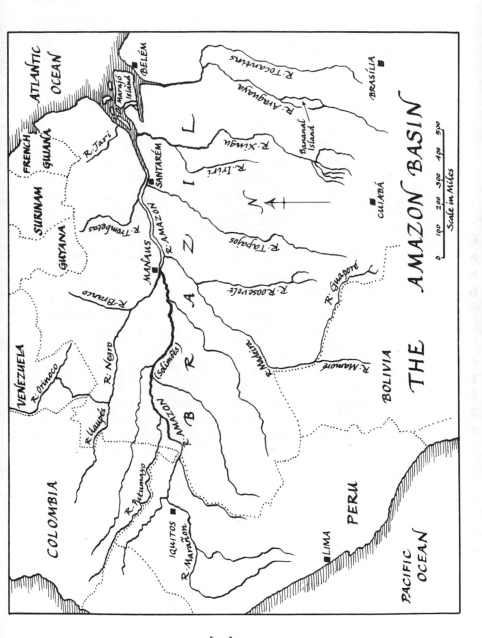

James to order the suspension of Captain North's plan to sail with the newly-commissioned Company fleet, on the grounds that the Spanish/Portuguese settlement at Belém do Pará constituted effective occupation of the whole Amazon basin.

Count Gondomar was assisted in his purpose of frustrating Sir Roger North's expedition by the efforts of Lord Digby, who was King James I's ambassador at the Spanish court and who—succumbing to one of the most insidious temptations to all diplomats resident abroad—was so preoccupied with the importance of good relations between his own country and his country of residence that he argued the Spanish case at home in disregard of other considerations. This he did to a point where at least one of his contemporaries* remarked:

> 'that he took the L. Digbie for the King of England's ambassador in Spaine, but yt seemed he is rather the K. of Spaine's ambassador in England'.

The outcome of all this pressure on the King was that North was ordered to hold his hand and not to sail for the Amazon. Such a postponement risked the whole enterprise aborting, because keeping the ships idle once they had been victualled and manned was excessively expensive. North therefore found himself in a quandary. The King had formally told him to postpone his sailing, but the King was known to be under pressure and his instructions might not necessarily reflect his true wishes. North's sponsors were restless at the delay. There was an influential party at court which 'expected him to go without bidding'. The members of the expedition were on the point of dispersing.

Not for nothing had North served under Raleigh and established a reputation as an independent adventurer. He took his fate into his own hands and on the 30th of April 1620 set sail from Plymouth for the Amazon without more ado.

Seven weeks later he reached the mouth of the river and

* John Chamberlain in a letter to Sir Dudley Carleton.

sailed straight on for a further 300 miles to the confluence of the Xingu river. Here he found the English and Irish who had remained behind since Roe's expedition of almost a decade before. He then sent one of his lieutenants—a certain William White—in a light 300-ton pinnace some 600 miles further up-stream, where he encountered numerous different Indian tribes which he described as 'manie Nations'.

North, like Roe before him, set up trading stations to deal in the commodities for which the Amazon was already becoming a recognized source: sugar cane, cotton, dyes, hard woods, gum, tobacco, coloured feathers, nutmeg and some other spices. As before also, the settlers persuaded the Indians to work contentedly for them, rewarding their services with such traditional inducements as knives and beads.

North doubtless felt he had achieved much and deserved recognition and reward. So, with a rich cargo of tobacco (hardly in itself likely to endear him to a King who had just published a *Counterblaste to Tobacco*) he left most of his expedition in well-established trading settlements with three of his smaller craft at their disposal, and set sail for England with some of those even earlier English settlers who had been there when he arrived in 1620 and who now felt that they were overdue for relief.

The passage home was slower and more perilous than the voyage out. By now his ship was showing signs of wear and tear: her sails and rigging had begun to rot in the tropical heat and the hull was springing leaks. So desperate was his condition on reaching the European coast of the Atlantic that he had to put in at the first available port, which—in the event—was a Spanish one. He was fortunate to be able to conceal his place of embarkation or he would never have been permitted to continue his voyage. But there his luck ran out. When he did get back to England it seemed he might as well have been exposed and detained in Spain: a warrant for his incarceration in the Tower was awaiting him.

Sir Roger North had known that he was taking a chance by sailing without the King's explicit authorization, but he had trusted that the passing of time, the success of his venture and the support of his backers would ensure an acclaimed return. But he had reckoned without Count Gondomar. When the Spanish Ambassador had first heard about North's surreptitious sailing he had protested; but when he heard about North's exultant return he made a scene at Whitehall the likes of which had not been seen since the time of Raleigh's clashes on the Orinoco. As before, King James was responsive to the Ambassador's tirades. At Gondomar's instigation, the unfortunate Lord North—whose only crime was that he was the brother of Sir Roger—was clapped in the Tower, and the Earl of Warwick was obliged to surrender the charter of the so-recently-formed Amazon Company and plead for a pardon for whatever offences its agents might have committed.

With his customary inconsistency, King James alternately imprisoned and released Sir Roger North for some months following the latter's return to the shores of England. The King also made difficulties for so long about the selling of North's cargo that the offending tobacco had deteriorated to such an extent that by the time it reached the market it was worth less than a shilling a pound. So, all in all, it looked in London as if Count Gondomar had won the day and the Amazon Company, its agents and its fortunes had all been brought effectively to an end.

But on the ground itself—that is on the banks of the Amazon 5000 miles away—the premature conclusion of the enterprise seemed a lot less sure. A string of English, Irish and Dutch settlements were scattered up the Amazon to a point beyond the confluence of the Tapajos river. There was even an occasional fort, as at Adriaansz near the mouth of the Xingu river.

These facts were not unknown in Madrid. And the Spanish court echoed Count Gondomar's concern that while these settlements lasted they had the possibility of expanding into a rival colony. Accordingly, the Spanish authorities, then dominating Portugal, sent out instructions that the English trading posts and forts left behind by North were to be sought out and destroyed. The task of reducing the English presence proved rather harder than had been expected because, unlike the Dutch, the English had not placed their settlements on the banks of the main stream of the Amazon or the Xingu but up narrow creeks and tributaries which were harder to find and easier to defend. Thus although by 1623 most of the Englishmen left behind by North had been killed, the community was not yet completely eliminated.

The most engaging of all the Anglo-Irish settlers whom North left behind was one Bernard O'Brien, who wrote a detailed account of his adventures. He established a fort some 250 miles up the Amazon with twelve Irishmen and four Englishmen, at a spot which they named Coconut Grove. O'Brien secured his base with wooden ramparts and earthworks, learnt the local Indian languages, traded goods with the Indians, and led them on punitive raids against their rival tribes. The Indians in turn laboured in the tobacco and cotton plantations and affected a willingness to adopt the Christian religion.

When the Portuguese harassment of the English settlements became a threat to his further existence where he was, O'Brien ventured even further into the interior: with five Irish musketeers and fifty Indians to paddle his canoes he sailed some further (unspecified) hundreds of miles upstream to where —with more imagination than credibility—he records how he met the Queen of the Amazons, Cuña Muchu, and bartered mirrors and lengths of Holland-cloth with her in return for women slaves and a safe-conduct even further upstream. O'Brien's circumstantial account of how the citizens of this entirely-female community had their 'right breasts small like men's, artificially stunted in order to shoot arrows, but the left breasts are broad like other women's' would have carried more conviction had these details not been available to him from the classical legend of the Amazons. He was not, of course, the first to make claims of such encounters: Francisco de Orellana, on his original voyage of discovery in 1540, had heard reports from the Indians of a ferocious female tribe and had claimed to have had contact with them—hence the naming of the river. But O'Brien's tale casts sufficient doubt over his veracity to have put in question much of the rest of his story were it not for the fact that there is corroborating evidence for at least some of his other more dramatic exploits.

Eventually even O'Brien was halted by hostile tribes who could not be bought off with mirrors, and he chose to follow an alternative river running northwards out of the Amazon—possibly the Trombetas; after various over-land portages, he linked up with the Surinam river and emerged eventually on the Atlantic coast, down which he travelled to the mouth of the Amazon, finally completing his circuit by going up the river again to return to Coconut Grove. But when by the following year, 1624, harassment by other European settlers—this time the Dutch—was still continuing, and still no reinforcements arrived, he left a compatriot called Philip Purcell in charge of his fort and plantations and himself returned to Europe. Soon after O'Brien had left, a Portuguese expedition sacked Coconut Grove and the prospects for any continued Anglo-Irish presence on the Amazon looked bleak indeed.

But this time the encouraging developments were at home. King James I had died and been succeeded by Charles I: the old era of suspicion of those exploring the Orinoco and Amazon rivers, and the old distaste for the tobacco trade, were past. Better still, from the point of view of the explorers, war had broken out between England and Spain: no longer would conflict and rivalry with Spanish and Portuguese settlers be frowned upon in London and result in being greeted on return home by warrants for incarceration in the Tower. The old

Amazon Company could not be resuscitated, but a new Guiana Company—subscribed to and supported by a galaxy of aristocratic names—was set up in the City of London in 1627.

The following year the Company sent out its first expedition: 112 colonists made a safe crossing and set up a settlement well into the Amazon estuary. They built a rectangular fort and—mindful of the fate of their predecessors—set about reinforcing it with 'an outer wall fifteen spans thick', a wooden palisade and a ditch. O'Brien too returned to the Amazon in 1629 and, on finding his old fort destroyed, built a new one for himself.

But the new enterprises were not to prosper. Reinforcements sent by the Guiana Company decided that life up the Amazon was too uncomfortable on account of the continued Portuguese harassment, and they decided to ignore their instructions and settle instead on the Wiapoco river in Guiana where—although there were less good profits to be made—life was quieter.

Nor was O'Brien's new establishment left long in peace. Pedro Teixeira, the intrepid Portuguese commander in Belém do Pará, had collected a formidable force of 120 Portuguese and 1600 Indians in 98 canoes and O'Brien, refusing an offer of help from the English settlers out of concern lest his Indian allies should be converted to Protestantism rather than Irish Catholicism, tried to negotiate a peace with the Portuguese. An instrument of surrender was elaborately drawn up 'in the name of the holy evangels with a missal, on our knees in front of a crucifix'. But, as John Hemming wryly remarks in his history of the Brazilian Indians*, 'some Holy symbol must have been missing', because the Portuguese no sooner had the Irish in their power than they stripped them not only of their money but of their clothes, murdered some of the prisoners and enslaved the others. O'Brien himself was put in chains and held as a prisoner for a year before being banished to live with a cannibal

* *Red Gold* (Macmillan 1978).

[27]

tribe. The Portuguese had proved themselves more interested in national than in religious domination of the Amazon basin.

No sooner had Teixeira disposed of the Irish than he turned his force on the English settlement on Tocujos Island in the Amazon estuary. Lacking the reinforcements which had absconded to the Wiapoco river, they too were vanquished. In 1630, a further English settlement under a robust military commander called Thomas Hixson fared no better: when one group tried to escape down the river from the Portuguese attack, the Indians in the Portuguese pay pursued them in canoes and splashed so hard with their paddles that the Englishmen's flintlocks were so wetted that they could not fire them; their arms thus rendered ineffective, the English were overpowered and slaughtered.

In 1631, a Captain Roger Fry, sent out by the Earl of Berkshire (an independent member of the Guiana Company), established himself at Fort Cumaú also in the estuary of the Amazon, but he too had been overwhelmed before he could be reinforced and was killed by the Portuguese together with 85 other compatriots. When the reinforcements did come the following year, they found Cunaú in ruins and the local Indians far too frightened of further Portuguese revenge to risk helping the newcomers. Without Indian help the English were hard pressed to feed themselves, and within two months 28 of the 40 in the party had died of starvation; the rest surrendered to the Portuguese. No further attempts were made to resuscitate the extinguished English settlements; by 1635 the Guiana Company had recognized that the Amazon was a lost cause to the British.

Why had this come about, when elsewhere the story was to be so different? The short answer must surely be that the implacable hostility of the Portuguese and Spanish combined was too much for the intruders. In the decades that followed, the English were to be more successful at establishing themselves in the face of similar hostility in the West Indies, but there were special strategic, geographical and logistical factors in their favour.* But on the Amazon the dice were loaded against the English: the Portuguese were there first, and the latter saw themselves as established by divine—or at least by Papal—authority under the treaty of Tordesillas; their numbers dominated throughout; they were determined on exclusivity. There was one very special reason for this last requirement: the routes bringing silver from the Spanish mines in Peru involved a particularly hazardous sea passage from Panama to Cuba, and thought was being given throughout the period to the possibility of using the Amazon as an alternative highway from Peru to the Atlantic; if that route were to become a practical possibility it would be essential that the whole river were in Spanish/Portuguese hands from source to sea; all intruders were potential pirates—as dangerous on the river as those other pirates already infesting the Caribbean; extermination was the only safe course.

But even despite these formidable factors, had the English entrepreneurs and explorers had the backing of their government—in the way in which the West Indian settlers were later to have the backing of Oliver Cromwell—they could perhaps have dislodged the Portuguese. The latter were based almost exclusively on one base; the port of Belém do Pará on the estuary of the Amazon. If James I or Charles I had been prepared to finance and equip an expedition against Belém, such as Cromwell was shortly to send against Jamaica, the whole course of the Amazon's history and development might have been changed. But James was too apprehensive of Spain, and Charles was too bedevilled by pecuniary worries following his quarrels with Parliament, and neither was imbued with the colonizing spirit of later times. The chance was irrevocably lost. From henceforth the English, and later the Americans, were to penetrate the green, lush world of the Amazon basin as outsiders only. And for many decades they were not to penetrate it at all.

* See the author's *The Quest for Captain Morgan* (Constable 1983).

2

THE ENQUIRERS

The later seventeenth and the eighteenth centuries were a closed chapter for the Amazon as far as the British were concerned, and indeed as far as most nationalities were concerned other than the Portuguese. The Portuguese military garrisons and the Portuguese Jesuit missionaries between them controlled the whole river from Belém to points far up the Solimões on the Spanish (now Peruvian) frontier, and far up the Rio Negro on the Spanish (now Colombian) frontier. An occasional foreigner was allowed to penetrate these private waters if he came with particularly good credentials or was particularly lucky: such a one was Charles de la Condamine, a French scientist sent by Louis XV to work on measuring the equator, who travelled the whole length of the river in the 1770s. But the English—despite their four-hundred-year-old European alliance with Portugal—did not qualify: as Protestants, they were viewed by the Jesuits with especial distaste.

By the end of the eighteenth century much had changed. The Jesuits had been expelled from all Portuguese domains at the instigation of the Marquis of Pombal; this meant the eventual closure of all their mission stations on the Amazon and elsewhere in Brazil. By the turn of the century the Portuguese metropolitan grip was itself to slacken: Napoleon's invasion of the Iberian peninsula led to the flight of the Portuguese royal family to Rio de Janeiro, which in turn led to the establishment of a separate imperial regime in Brazil in the early years of the nineteenth century. The way was not immediately open for foreign visitors to the Amazon; civil disturbances culminated in 1835 in open war between the

Portuguese settlers and the *cabanos* (or native peasants of Pará), but by 1840 this too had been brought to a bloody end. It now emerged that, as an independent country, Brazil was no longer to be as paranoiac about the activities of foreigners as she had been as a European colony.

Furthermore, just as Brazil was becoming more accessible, so the urge to explore—on the part of the Anglo-Saxon races at least—was becoming more pronounced. The romantic movement in Europe had awakened an enthusiasm for the wildest manifestations of nature, be they the Swiss Alps, the deserts of Egypt or the forests of the Amazon. Simultaneously, the study of natural history, which was an off-shoot of the scientific progress of the eighteenth century, was bounding into the age of Darwin. Baron von Humboldt had made his celebrated journeys of scientific discovery to the Amazon and Orinoco basins at the turn of the eighteenth and nineteenth centuries, and published his influential findings on 'the equinoctial regions of America' throughout the second and third decades of the nineteenth century.

Apart from a rather disingenuous Englishman—Charles Waterton—who made a number of expeditions mostly north of the Amazon between 1812 and 1824, the most notable Anglo-Saxons on the Amazon in the first years of the nineteenth century were usually young naval officers. In the 1820s, Henry Maw left his ship on the Pacific coast of Peru and travelled over the Andes and down virtually the whole length of the navigable Amazon; in the following decade two more Royal Naval officers—Lieutenants Smyth and Lowe—made virtually the same journey. They all had adventures, and they all wrote them up in lively accounts which Mr John Murray of Albermarle Street, who was already making a name for himself not only as a publisher of Lord Byron's popular narrative poems of travel but also of the prose works of less lyrical travellers, was happy to put out over his imprint.

But the traveller whose account was to excite immediate and

influential successors was in fact an American. William H. Edwards came from New York City and had his interest aroused in the region on account of having a relative in the American consulate in Buenos Aires. In 1846 Edwards found himself expressing what many were to conclude:

'In these stirring times, when all Anglo-Saxondom is on the qui-vive for novelty . . . it has been a matter of surprise to me that those who live upon the excitement of seeing and telling some new thing have so seldom betaken themselves to our Southern continent.'

Edwards therefore decided to set off and put this to rights. Never one to shirk superlatives or colourful phrases, he directed himself to the region where

'the mightiest of rivers rolls majestically through primeval forests of boundless extent . . . where gold has tempted, and Amazonian women repulsed, the unprincipled adventurer; and where Jesuit missionaries, and luckless traders, have fallen victims to cannibal Indians and epicurean anacondas.'

Having reached his supposedly alarming destination, Edwards spent some weeks in Belém and then set off on a forty-day passage up the Amazon and the Rio Negro, determined—in his own words—'to have a jolly cruise'; he persevered until a point which he concluded was 'higher than any American had ever been before'. Although he explicitly made no pretensions to be a naturalist, he collected specimens of animal, insect and vegetable life whenever he could manage to secure something which he considered unusual; and he wrote a lively account of his four-month experience in a book* which John Murray published in London the following year.

* It was predictably entitled *A Voyage up the River Amazon.*

Sir Walter Raleigh, whose explorations of the
Orinoco inspired his captains to explore the Amazon,
with his son Wat who was killed on the Orinoco.

Sir Thomas Roe who sailed up the Amazon in 1610 and founded English settlements there.

Fortifications such as these at Belém effectively prevented foreign incursions on the Amazon for most of the 17th and 18th centuries.

A R Wallace, the English
naturalist and friend of
Darwin, who spent years
on the Amazon classifying
new species.

H A Wickham who
purloined the Amazonia
rubber seeds that were t
be the foundation of the
Malayan rubber industr

Carajas Indians on
Aragayan river: Richard
Spruce mistrusted such
'shirted Indians'.

River travel has changed little over the centuries:
above, under sail off Marajo Island at the mouth of
the Amazon and, below, under paddle three
thousand miles upstream.

Abandoned engines beside the jungle track of the
Madeira/Mamoré railway, built at heavy cost in lives.

Roger Casement
April 17, 19

Sir Roger Casement whose
report on the murder, rape
and exploitation of the
Indians by the rubber barons
caused a sensation in
London.

Colonel Theodore Roosevelt
who, as an ex-President of
the United States, nearly
died discovering a tributary
of the Amazon that now
bears his name.

The book was not an outstanding one by any criterion: Edwards's literary abilities were pedestrian, his adventures unremarkable, and his scientific observations either non-existent or very amateur. But it served as a trigger to other and far more spectacular achievements: 'Mr Edwards' little book' caught the eye of Alfred Russel Wallace, who—unlike Edwards—was a very serious naturalist indeed, and was to become a close associate of Darwin's in developing the theory of evolution. Wallace in turn was in touch with Henry Walter Bates, another promising naturalist, and suggested to him a joint expedition to the Amazon to gather material and facts 'towards solving the problem of the origin of the species'. The two men met in London early in 1848 and, after nosing round the sparse collections of South American flora and fauna that existed, decided that they would set out together in April of that year and make their own collections—paying their expenses by selling off their duplicate specimens to museums and collectors all over Europe.

The third of the great British naturalists who were to spend many overlapping years on the Amazon was Richard Spruce. After a period as a young schoolmaster in Yorkshire, he—like Wallace—had been early attracted to Darwin's writings about South America; he had travelled to Spain as a full-time botanist, living off the sale of Pyrenean plants, and eventually securing a post at Kew Gardens. Then, in 1849, he set sail for his longed-for objective—the Amazon—on the same ship as Wallace's younger brother.

It was a good moment for pioneer naturalists from the English-speaking world to set out, for they were breaking fresh ground: what few earlier zoologists, biologists and botanists there had been in the first years of the nineteenth century were continentals such as von Spix and von Martius or Count de Castelnau. It was a virgin field—or rather a virgin forest—for Anglo-Saxons.

For the next few years all three naturalists—Wallace, Bates

and Spruce—were to work and travel on the banks of the
Amazon and its tributaries: Bates penetrating far up the
Solimões, Wallace far up the Rio Negro and Uaupés, and
Spruce on all these rivers as well as crossing over the head-
waters of the Amazon into Ecuador. For some time Wallace
and Bates worked together and on rare occasions, as at
Santarém at the end of 1849, all three men met at the same
place.

They had much in common. They were all struggling
financially as well as physically to keep themselves on the
Amazon, and living by selling specimens. It was hardly a
lucrative business: Bates's agent gave him fourpence a specimen and took twenty per cent commission on the deal; another
five per cent was taken by remittance charges and the cost of
the boxes for the specimens. His total profit for the work of one
year and eight months (he recorded in his journal on 20 March
1851) had been just £26 and 19 shillings. In the circumstances
they seldom managed to make much savings, and even when
they did these were precarious. Spruce, when he had finally
accumulated a capital of £700 after twelve years of incessant
collecting, lost it all owing to the failure of the bank at
Guayaquil with whom he had deposited it.

Bates's description of the financial mechanics of living on
the Amazon would have applied equally to all of them. The
agent in London, to whom he despatched his specimens, sent
him drafts cashable with an English trading house at Belém.
When he went up-country he found that the Portuguese or
Brazilian traders would—in turn—cash his drafts on the
English trading house in Belém. If caught short by the failure
of his drafts to arrive from England, these traders would give
him advances, without interest, until his funds came through
—such was the credit of an English nineteenth-century
gentleman traveller. In the few towns up the river, English
sovereigns or American, Spanish and Mexican dollars were all
acceptable, and Spruce found he could change English five

pound notes into local currency with no difficulty in Belém. When it came to travelling further into Indian territory up the higher tributaries, currency of any denomination was useless and goods for barter had to be procured in advance. Bates records that all travellers on the branch rivers had to take cloth and *caxaça* (the local potable alcohol); and Wallace records that he took

'bales of coarse cotton cloth and of the commonest calico, of flimsy but brilliantly coloured prints, of checked or striped cottons, and of blue and red handkerchiefs . . . axes and cutlasses, pointed knives in great profusion, fish-hooks by thousands, flints and steels, gunpowder, shot, quantities of blue, black and white beads, and countless little looking-glasses.'

All three explorer naturalists started by spending several months at Belém and studying flora and fauna of the hinterland of this port at the mouth of the great river. All three thereafter equipped themselves for extensive river travel in the far interior of the country. The journey for the first thousand miles up to the mouth of the River Negro at Manaus was originally made by a swift sailing *galliota* manned with an additional dozen Indian paddlers. But Bates records that during his first years on the Amazon, Indian crews and paddlers were getting ever scarcer and less reliable. Even Brazilian senior officials, such as judges and military commandants had to travel by trading vessels. These heavier sailing ships progressed well up-stream while the east wind blew, but when the wind dropped they were reduced to progress by means of a curiously cumbersome process known as *espia*: this involved sending the ship's boat ahead with a couple of hands to secure a cable to a stout tree and then handling the ship up to the tree and starting all over again. By this method a voyage to Manaus which would have taken forty days by fast *galliota* often took three months in the wet season, when the winds had dropped and the river was swollen with the fast current of flood waters rolling down to the sea. In 1850, Spruce was at Santarém when, in two days, the Amazon rose forty feet; he recorded that water spread for four hundred miles on either side of the main channels; plantations were inundated; 'great masses of green islands filled the river'.

But above Manaus, particularly further up the Rios Negro, Uaupés, Blanco and Solimões, it was by canoe that one travelled. Spruce always preferred this as he felt he was 'master of his own movements' and could stop where and when he liked. He also managed to make himself comfortable on the canoes. He had two cabin areas erected: that in the stern was 'long enough to suspend my hammock within it' and allowed him to range his collecting boxes along the sides to act as tables and seats, with his rifle slung from the palm-thatched roof; that in the bow kept the stores and barter goods dry. Wallace had exactly the same arrangement. Usually such canoes—known as *cobertas* on account of the covered areas—were about twenty-four feet long and about eight feet wide; they also had masts and sails which could be rigged if there were a steady favourable wind; the crew would consist of some half-dozen Indians.

The canoes were generally handled well even in rough rapids, but there were occasional mishaps: a Mr Graham, described by Edwards as a 'wealthy manufacturer from England', was drowned in an upset with all his family, and Spruce found that 'when the river began to be obstructed by rocks and the current to run furiously . . . instead of working among my plants, I had to watch over the safety of the canoe'. The cataracts around São Gabriel on the Uaupés were particularly rough and ill-famed and Spruce resorted to being hauled up the edge from boulder to boulder.

There was, of course, a strict limit to the amount of provisions which even the best constructed canoe, complete with forward cabin, could accommodate. Each of the travellers had

[36]

their own ideas about the most vital necessities. Only Edwards, travelling on a comfortable 30-foot *galliota* which he himself described as 'a sort of pleasure craft', went in for luxuries. He found room for 'some pots of New York oysters, bought from a clever captain in Pará harbour . . . sundry demi-johns of wine, Yankee dough-nuts, tin cases of cheese and all the usual supplies'. The usual supplies were, in fact, considerably more frugal and consisted in Wallace's case of *'farinha* (flour), fish and *caxaça* for the men; with the addition of tea, coffee, biscuits, sugar, rice, salt beef and cheese for ourselves'. When setting off from Barra for the upper reaches of the Rio Negro on what he thought might be up to a year's absence from civilization, Wallace added brandy, for medicinal purposes, garlic, black pepper and some extra *caxaça* for his own consumption 'and other little household luxuries' which included a live turkey for later roasting. Bates and Spruce give very similar lists. Clearly most of the dietary variety had to be provided by hunting and fishing as they went.

Provisions were not, of course, the only things for which room had to be found in the canoes. Edwards complained that before setting out from New York he had not been able to get any reliable information about the sort of equipment he should take; he therefore included in his book a list as a guide to his successors, and no doubt Wallace at least—having been inspired by the book in the first place—took it fairly seriously. It is a splendidly comprehensive document and gives one a good idea of what was stowed in all those lockers in the forward cabin area. Possibly 'the black suit . . . required by Pará etiquette' might have been left behind, but certainly the 'half dozen suits of light material, some of which are calculated for forest wear' would not have been. Nor would the 'check and flannel shirts'—considered so good for fevered travellers. The 'well filled medicine chest' included Hartshorn, a remedy 'more valuable than ought else, being effective against the stings of all insects'. Powder and fine shot were to be taken for hunting, and a variety of naturalists' impedimenta such as arsenic, flower-presses, as well as paper and wooden boxes 'for insects and other objects'. Finally, a poncho-cape of heavy cloth lined with baize was recommended not only against rain but as bedding and pillow. Bates when he set out for three months on the upper reaches of the Solimões added a tent of mosquito netting, under which he could sling his hammock. But on the whole Edwards's list was the best guide and retained its relevance for Amazonian travellers for at least a century.

Having got themselves to the Amazon, made their financial arrangements, stocked up with stores and barter goods, and set in hand arrangements for river travel, how did the naturalists spend their days? They have left some very explicit accounts, perhaps the clearest being Bates's description of a typical day at Belém where he passed nearly a year and a half before he set off on his more perilous travels up-river. His routine was precise. He rose at dawn and spent two hours before breakfast on ornithology; this was the time of day when he was sure to see toucans, parrots and other exotic varieties. After breakfast he got down to the serious business of the day: –

'Between 9 and 10 a.m. I prepare for the woods . . . over my left shoulder slings my double-barrelled gun, loaded, one with No. 10, one with No. 4 shot. In my right hand I take my net; on my left side . . . is suspended my insect box . . . on my right side hangs my game bag, with thongs to hang lizards, snakes, frogs or large birds; one small pocket contains . . . damped cork for the micro-lepidoptera; to my shirt is pinned my pincushion, with six sizes of pins.'

After all this meticulous panoply was assembled, the conscientious naturalist sallied forth again—this time bent on entomology, for which the optimum time, he records, was 'a little before the greatest heat of the day—92° or 93° Fahr.' Within an hour of his lodgings outside Belém he found he could encounter 700 different species of butterflies (as compared —he points out—to the 66 different species known in England, or the 390 in all Europe). At sundown he would return home 'fatigued with our ramble', to an evening spent in sorting out his latest finds and making notes about them.

Wallace, when up-country, undertook a tougher routine. He rose about 5.30 a.m. and skinned birds and monkeys, brought in overnight or shot by him at dawn, until breakfasting off Indian porridge. Then he too set off, net in hand, for a long day in the forest, returning in the evening to dine off cow-fish or the meat of deer which he had bagged earlier in the day.

Spruce, being more concerned than the others with plants and trees, had a particularly frustrating time: all the best specimens were high above the forest floor as everything reached for the sun. He could not always find agile Indians to shin up 100-foot trees to take cuttings of flowers, fruit and leaves, so he was reduced to cutting down 'magnificent trees, perhaps centuries old, merely for the sake of getting flowers'. Hours were often spent in felling a single tree. After a long morning of hunting, felling and collecting, Spruce would often spend the heat of the afternoon stifling in his hammock under the stern covering of his canoe, and then, after taking a bath (not a bathe) in the river, would fish for his supper in the cool of the evening while he listened to the howling of the surrounding monkeys.

These routines, whether in a forest camp near Belém, in some smaller jungle settlement up-country, or on a canoe up some remote creek, were scrupulously maintained. The day was parcelled out between the different scientific objectives. The sundowner of *caxaça* was drunk. The 'forest suits' were washed by the Indians. The butterfly pins were arranged in the pincushions. Just as much as their Victorian contemporaries who were setting out their orderly lines of tents on the corpse-strewn plains of the Crimea, or continuing their daily rounds through the privations of the siege of Lucknow (both the Crimean War and the Indian Mutiny took place while Bates and Spruce were still up the Amazon), these essentially English Englishmen kept up their own self-imposed standards and disciplines under the most un-English conditions.

Of course, not all Englishmen—even in such a remote quarter of the globe as the Amazon—preserved the codes of conduct expected of their race. Spruce had the misfortune to enlist a thoroughly bad hat as his assistant in Manaus in 1855: Charles Nelson, lately of the Royal Navy, had been drawn to the Amazon by talk of gold there. He appeared to Spruce as a tough, strong compatriot who would be useful in helping to make camps and manage canoes and occasionally drunken Indians up-country. What Spruce did not know when he hired him was that Nelson had already been arrested in Peru for murder and had an uncontrollable temper. He fought with everyone up the Solimões and obliged Spruce to sleep with a pistol in his hammock for self-defence. When eventually Spruce discharged him, giving him three months' wages and his fare back to Manaus, Nelson never got there: the Indians fell on him on his jungle trail and hacked him to pieces. It required a particular type of Englishman or American to survive in this hostile environment.

Indeed, one of the most characteristically Victorian of their attitudes was that adopted towards the Indians. The pure Indian was considered a noble savage, to be respected and trusted; but the half-caste or semi-civilized Indian was to be despised and mistrusted. Spruce spoke for all of them when he wrote 'God save me from Indians with shirts'; he would never voluntarily employ any Indian who had been introduced to European practices or made ashamed of his nakedness. Nor would he employ half-castes, 'for the least streak of white blood in an Indian's veins increases tenfold his insolence and insubordination'. Wallace also attributed the deceits and desertions practised on him at São Jeronymo on the Uaupés to the fact that the only helpers he could get there as interpreters, hunters and paddlers were 'half-civilized Indians with a taste for *caxaça*'.

Spruce had two distinctly dangerous and unpleasant incidents with his Indians. At the small village of São Carlos on the Rio Negro, on the border of Brazil and Venezuela, in 1853, Spruce was warned by Portuguese settlers that the local Indians—who, needless to say, were of the 'shirted' or half-caste variety—intended to massacre the few white inhabitants on the feast-day of St John. Flight was recommended. Spruce had not yet collected all the specimens he wanted from the local trees. So instead of fleeing he put his temporary house into a state fit to resist attack or siege: windows were barred; slits for firing through were opened up; water and food were stored; the most apprehensive of the Portuguese took turns with him in keeping watch. In the event, a good deal of random firing was indulged in, but no massacre attempted. Spruce continued calmly with his cataloguing and only moved on when he had exhausted the local flora.

The second incident was more personal and alarming. The following year, in 1854, when returning down the Rio Negro from São Carlos towards Manaus, his crew of four Indians started plotting to kill him, being under the mistaken impression that his little parcels of plants were trade goods with which they would make off once they had disposed of Spruce. They calculated that since Spruce was already known to be a sick man—he was recovering from an unusually severe bout of malaria—his death and disappearance would arouse little subsequent investigation. Spruce heard them plotting at night as he lay fevered in his hammock. The Indians were used to his leaving the hammock regularly (he had mild dysentery as well as malaria) and so were confident he would return when he walked off into the forest; in fact, he made for the canoe and barricaded himself with his shot-gun behind a bulwark of plant samples for the rest of the night. By morning, realizing that

Spruce had got wind of something and was fully armed and alert, the Indians had lost either courage or cupidity: they paddled him on peacefully down stream.

The fact that Spruce had been ill was in no way unusual. All the early explorers of the Amazon spent a great deal of their time suffering from a variety of serious and often deadly ailments. An outbreak of yellow fever in Belém was probably the worst peril for the naturalists. It carried off Wallace's younger brother who had come out to join him on the Amazon, and very nearly Bates too, who nursed the younger Wallace at considerable risk to himself and then succumbed to a milder form of the same fever—from which he recovered after massive doses of Epsom Salts. Spruce was up-river at Santarém during the outbreak and suffered nothing worse than a suspension of supplies from Belém. Wallace was much further up-stream at Barra when he heard—too late—the news of his brother's fatal attack of yellow fever; within days he had himself succumbed to a different fever for which he was dosing himself liberally with quinine and 'cream of tartar water', though he was so weak he could hardly minister to himself and wrote that 'it is at such times that one feels the want of a friend or attendant, for of course it is impossible to get the Indians to do these little things without so much explanation and showing as would require more exertion than doing them oneself.' Before he was fully recovered from what turned out to be a recurring ague, he found his Indians had been taking advantage of his weakness to drink the *caxaça* he had brought for preserving fishes.

Yellow fever and undefined agues were not the only hazards. Bates found leprosy rife in Santarém, and malaria was a constant threat and a regular occurrence. Spruce was struck so severely with malaria at Esmeralda that his life was in danger for 38 days and his Indians had sold most of his equipment to buy rum for themselves before a passing Portuguese trader took compassion on him and gave him a passage down-stream and back into Brazil. Dysentery, attributed frequently to eating the river fish, was never long absent. The cumulative effect of all this sickness and fever was debilitating: Bates ended his book by remarking that his current ague 'seemed to be the culmination of a gradual deterioration of health which had been going on for several years . . . I had exposed myself too much . . .' But on they struggled: shivering fits, agues, fevers . . . all were treated stoically with quinine—'as much as would lie on the tip of a penknife-blade, mixed with a little warm chamomile tea'.

Apart from the dangers from Indians and diseases there was also—of course—the ever-present menace of the wild life itself. The most impressive examples of this were the jaguars which occasionally crossed their path: Wallace was 'walking quietly along' on the banks of the Rio Negro when a large jet-black jaguar appeared 20 yards ahead of him on the path; he raised his gun to his shoulder and then recalled that both barrels were loaded with small shot—effective for shooting birds for the pot but calculated only to enrage a jaguar. The jaguar regarded Wallace thoughtfully and strode on, causing a scampering of small animals out of its path through the forest. Bates was jealous of his luck as he had hoped to see a jaguar: he records that they so alarmed his men, by roaring close to his camp on one occasion, that the Indians lit fires around the outside of the camp (in the hope these would keep the jaguar away) and Bates sat up half the night (in the hope the jaguar might come to 'warm themselves'). Both were unsuccessful: spoor marks in the morning showed that the jaguars had —undeterred—tramped around the camp, but Bates had seen nothing.

But if sighting of jaguar was a rare occurrence, the same was not true of snakes. Bates tells how his canoe was attacked at night by an anaconda which hammered a hole in the chicken coop on board with its head, and then ate a couple of hens; the subsequent hunt for the anaconda revealed that it was 'not a very large specimen' being a mere 18 feet 9 inches in length and 16 inches in circumference. A few days later he encountered a boa-constrictor whose 'rapidly moving and shining body looked like a stream of brown liquid'; he pursued it in the hope of being able to note its size and markings and was disappointed when he lost it in 'a dense swampy thicket'. On another occasion, Wallace gives a matter of fact account of capturing a 'fine young boa-constrictor' on the veranda of the house where he was staying, but having difficulty catching enough live rats to keep it in good fettle. Considerably more dangerous than anaconda or boa-constrictor was the Jararáca, with its hideous flat triangular head and four-inch-long poison fangs, and with its bite which Wallace—not given to exaggeration—described as 'certain death' and Bates—who also encountered one—described as being responsible for four or five deaths in his own experience. Typically, Bates deeply regretted the killing of the one he encountered at close quarters before he had a chance to examine it 'as a specimen'. Scientific curiosity could always be depended upon to get the better of fear or revulsion with Bates or Wallace.

Alligators always provide the largest number of horror stories for Amazonian travellers, and Bates, Wallace and Spruce were no exceptions. Bates stumbled on the remains of one which had just been largely devoured by a jaguar—characteristically, his only reaction was disappointment at having missed the encounter. On another occasion he was regaled by one of his men telling him how his son had been dragged under water by an alligator which had been forced to release the boy when the father had pursued it through the water and thrust his fingers into the beast's eyes: the boy displayed the tooth marks on his thigh to verify the story. Wallace witnessed what can only be described as an alligator drive: negro beaters with long poles forced a large quantity of alligators into the bank where they were harpooned or lassoed, dragged ashore and then attacked with axes; the 'bag' amounted to fifty on the first day and thirty more the following day; the inducement to all this slaughter being the fat which was extracted from them rather than their skins. At a different time Wallace relished eating alligator meat—the tail being the best part—which he described as having 'a very strong but rather agreeable odour, like guavas or some musky fruit'. When they were not coping with jaguars, snakes or alligators, there were sting rays, vampire bats and sauba ants to arouse their professional curiosity rather than their apprehension.

To the Indians they encountered, such men as Bates, Wallace and Spruce must have seemed strange, unreal figures. But even to their fellow Englishmen, they must have appeared curiously eccentric. Spruce was a fine linguist and had an easy manner with the Indians which contrasted with a stilted and formal manner with his fellow Europeans; he was less self-conscious casting off his shoes and dancing to the drums of the Indians, than he was wearing his black suit among the expatriates in Belém. He was accompanied for much of his travels by a large mongrel dog called Sultan, whom he had brought up from a puppy. Sultan was a staunch companion through most of the adversities of jungle travel, but was allergic to rapids and whirlpools; when caught in the latter while descending the Rio Huallaga by canoe, Sultan finally got so put off water that he refused ever to drink again. Spruce was distraught; he sat beside the ailing, panting dog for days, trying to tempt him to drink, but finally he had to shoot him. It was the only time the Indians saw him weep.

Wallace was also fairly eccentric and rather donnish in his ways. For a man who spent so much time with firearms at the ready, he was strangely inept in their use. He dropped his gun into the river while duck-shooting and 'hooked it up again' still loaded on one occasion, and a few days later committed an even more careless offence when his gun

[45]

'was lying loaded on top of the canoe, and wishing to shoot some small birds, I drew it towards me by the muzzle, which, standing on the steps of the landing place, was the only part that I could reach. The hammer however lay in a joint of the boards, and as I drew the gun towards me it was raised up, and let fall on the cap, firing off the gun, the charge carrying off a small piece of the under-side of my hand, near the wrist, and, passing under my arm within a few inches of my body, luckily missed a number of people who were behind me. I felt my hand violently blown away, and looking at it, saw a stream of blood . . .'

One feels Wallace might not have been a favourite guest at Victorian shooting parties in the Shires.

Inevitably one wonders what was the ultimate achievement of so many years spent in the wilds of the Amazon, of so many discomforts endured and of so many hazards survived. In quantitative terms certainly, there was a formidable achievement: Bates alone collected over 14,000 different species of insects on the Amazon, of which 8,000 were new to science. Spruce sent back over 30,000 plant specimens to Kew Gardens and was also sending specimens of plants to London, Edinburgh, Dublin, St Petersburg, Vienna, Paris, Budapest, Brussels, Munich, Gottingen and Berlin. But more important than all this classification and collection were the new ideas which resulted from their discoveries. Bates was the first to develop the theory of protective mimicry. Spruce brought a trained scientific intelligence to the assessment of native herbal traditions and remedies, and found some of them well-based; he also did work on the development of Cinchona trees and bark for the more productive extraction of quinine, which was to have a marked effect on the health of the British army in India. Spruce—as a side-line and hobby—classified twenty-one vocabularies of Amazonian Indians, and mapped much of the 10,000 miles of river and stream which he had navigated.

[46]

But the most influential and far-reaching of all the theses to emerge from this Amazonian travel was Wallace's work on the theory of evolution. Second only in significance to the work of Darwin, who was in regular correspondence with both Wallace and Bates, Wallace would perhaps have become as prominent as Darwin had it not been for his self-effacing character and religious scruples about some aspects of the implications of his theory.

It was little wonder that Bates became the first paid official of the Royal Geographical Society in London and also a fellow of the Royal Society, that Spruce—though subsisting into old age on a pitifully small pension—was given a doctorate by the Imperial German Academy, and that Wallace, who survived until 1913, came to be viewed as one of the venerable old men of British scientific life. Between the three of them they had spent 32 years up the Amazon, and had got to know it better than any Anglo-Saxon had ever done before. But they had always felt themselves to be intruders there—never safe, never secure, never at home—as their countrymen had felt themselves to be before and would feel themselves to be again thereafter.

3

THE RAIDER

It was not many years before these gentle English naturalists, with their butterfly nets and their ammonia bottles, were to be followed down the Rio Negro and the Amazon by another Englishman of a more thrusting character, whose motivation was less concerned with knowledge for its own sake than with the profitable consequences of such knowledge.

Henry Alexander Wickham, like the botanists who preceded him, came from a professional middle class English family, but he had had a hard upbringing. His father—a London lawyer —had died when he was only four years old, and his mother had had to bring him up on the proceeds of working in a milliner's shop in Sackville Street. This had not prevented him from studying art and becoming a very competent draughts-man. Like many young Victorians, he yearned for adventure and set out in the 1860s for the Caribbean and Central America. He became fascinated by the Orinoco River and eventually made a memorable journey 'by way of the great cataracts of the Orinoco, Atabapo and Rio Negro' to a point on the Amazon near Santarém. He wrote an account of his adventures, charmingly illustrated with his own pen and ink drawings, which was published in London in 1872 entitled *Rough Notes of a Journey through the Wilderness*. So far there had been nothing to distinguish him very much from his predecessors.

But while Bates, Wallace and Spruce had thought little beyond the possible medical applications of the botanical knowledge they were revealing, Wickham's mind turned into more commercial channels. He noted that 'the highlands about the head of the (river) Branco will probably be one of the richest . . . districts of Equatorial America, when once fairly opened by enterprise'; and he went on to comment on the prospects of rounding up wild cattle and bringing them into Manaus where they 'would immediately realize a large sum'. He concluded his account of his travels by affirming that 'turn which way you will in this, the greatest water valley of the world, there seems to be an unlimited opening for enterprise or capital'.

He decided to practise what he preached and settled at Santarém—some half way between Manaus and the mouth of the Amazon—and started growing a variety of crops: tobacco, tapioca, sugar and eventually rubber. It was his experiments with this last product that led him into the adventure for which he is remembered.

In the rarefied atmosphere of the India Office in London, a very different type of man—Clements Markham—was also turning his mind to rubber, and more particularly to the need for this product in the expanding British Empire. Markham was an energetic official in his thirties, who had started life in the Royal Navy (taking part in the expedition of 1850 to relieve Sir John Franklin in the Arctic) and had then left the Navy to travel in Peru*. Here he had spotted the medicinal qualities of quinine and had shared with Spruce the credit for introducing this drug to India. After that achievement it was natural that he should be on the lookout for other products which could profitably thrive in India; and rubber—though tyres were not to be the main requirement for half a century to come—was needed to cope with the insulating and shock-absorbing

---

* He was to pursue his interests in travel and the Empire for a further sixty years after leaving the Navy, becoming secretary and later president of the Royal Geographical Society and receiving a knighthood from Queen Victoria. He lived to learn of the death of Captain Scott in Antarctica in 1912, and his copious diaries and note books have recently been acquired by the RGS.

requirements of the steam age. Where better could it be grown for the needs of the British Empire than in British India? Markham was in touch with Dr Joseph Hooker, the director of the Royal Botanical Gardens at Kew outside London, and determined that together they should identify and import the best wild rubber seed. This they found to be the *hevea brasiliensis* which produced the 'Pará Fine Hard' rubber of which Britain was already importing a sizeable crop from Brazil every year. And, by great good fortune, Hooker was already in correspondence with Wickham who—by 1873 —was firmly established at Santarém in the very heart of the *hevea* rubber country.

What Markham and Hooker required was a large quantity of the seeds which could be propagated in the hothouse conditions of Kew and then exported as seedlings and young plants to the most promising quarters of the Empire in the Indian sub-continent and the Far East. There were three problems: first, collecting enough of the seeds, which required a large-scale operation on the Amazon which might attract unwelcome attention locally; secondly, getting the seeds out of Brazil when the Brazilian authorities were already aware of the value of their world monopoly of this valuable crop; and thirdly, getting the seeds safely across the Atlantic before they had rotted or otherwise deteriorated beyond further propagation. It was a tall order to impose on a single individual in alien surroundings, with no organization behind him nor funds at his disposal —even if the individual was an adventurer and entrepreneur at heart.

Wickham's first consideration was to ensure that the game was worth the candle. He did nothing until he had negotiated terms with Hooker of Kew, who in turn had to negotiate with Markham of the India Office, who in turn had to negotiate with those who controlled the purse-strings of the Raj. Eventually it was agreed that Wickham should receive ten pounds sterling for every thousand seeds. More negotiations resulted in a firm order for sufficient quantities to make Wickham feel that it was worth his while to mount a major operation up the tributaries of the Tapajós river in 1876.

He therefore addressed himself to the first of his problems: how to collect so many seeds without arousing suspicions and hostility. Here Wickham benefited from the earlier activities of Bates, Wallace and Spruce. He let it be known up and down the river that he was yet another eccentric English naturalist —different only from his predecessors in that he had funds with which amply to reimburse those who did his collecting for him. In his own account*, he describes how:

'Working with as many Tapuyo Indians as I could get together at short notice, I daily ranged the forest, and packed on our backs in Indian pannier baskets as heavy loads of seed as we could march down under. I was working against time'.

The reason he was in a hurry was that he had—by a remarkable stroke of luck and cheek—managed to find a possible solution to the third of his problems: how to get whatever seeds he collected across the Atlantic so fast that they did not rot or deteriorate. An English ship—'a fully equipped ocean liner'—belonging to the newly-formed Inman line and called the *S. S. Amazonas* had arrived at Santarém on its first direct voyage from Liverpool to the upper Amazon. Wickham had been among those invited to dine on the ship and had found the occasion to be 'an altogether unlooked-for good evening on board, with a well-appointed supper in the saloon'. He had struck up a convivial and friendly relationship with the master—Captain Murray. The *Amazonas* had then sailed on up river.

But a few days later 'the startling news came down the river

* *On the plantation, cultivation and curing of Para Indian rubber, with an account of its introduction from the West to the Eastern Tropics* (London 1908).

[51]

that our fine ship the *Amazonas* had been abandoned, and left on the captain's hands, after having been stripped by the two gentlemen super cargoes (our late hospitable entertainers!) and that without so much as a stick of cargo for return voyage to Liverpool.' What appears to have happened was that the company's officials in charge of selling the outward cargo and purchasing a new cargo for the voyage home had fulfilled the first part of their obligation, but had then pocketed the proceeds and decamped in Manaus without making a provision for financing the return voyage. Captain Murray and his brand new ship were in a fix.

Henry Wickham was quick to see the captain's dilemma as his own opportunity. He relished the moment to make a bold decision:

> 'Then occurred one of those chances, such as a man has to take at top-side or lose for ever . . . I determined to plunge for it.'

With no funds at his disposal, with no authority from Dr Hooker or Clements Markham, and with little enough reason to think that the parsimonious India Office would back him, he informed the perplexed Captain Murray that he was chartering the *S. S. Amazonas* on behalf of the government of India to do a rapid transatlantic crossing with an undefined cargo which he, Wickham, would provide. At a stroke he had his means of getting the rubber seeds quickly to Kew.

All he did not have were the rubber seeds: hence his mobilization of all the Indians he could get together to work against time at collecting them. Despite his hurry, Wickham had to ensure that the work was not done hastily nor carelessly. He got the Tapoyo 'village maids' to make up open-work baskets of split cane to carry the seeds down to the waiting canoes on the river; but the baskets had to be lined with banana leaves between each layer of seed and Wickham was very conscious of the risk that if the leaves were not properly dried then the seeds would rot. It was a situation where too much rushing of the Indians would ruin the whole operation, and too little would result in missing the *rendez-vous* with Captain Murray.

Wickham's familiarity with the region, with the language, with other planters and with the Indian tappers stood him in good stead. They must have thought him a somewhat fevered naturalist as he led his teams scavenging seeds up and down the Tapajós-crossing which he described as 'rather ticklish work in a small canoe at that season'. By the time the *Amazonas* had returned to Santarém from her unhappy experience further up-river at Manaus, Wickham had 70,000 seeds ready to embark.

Now his priority was solving the second of his original three problems: how to get the seeds past the Brazilian authorities and out of Brazil. No actual law existed against the exportation of rubber seeds at that time. Indeed the Commercial Museum at Belém became so incensed by suggestions that the *hevea brasiliensis* had been illegally allowed to reach the outside world through the incompetence or corruption of their own state officials that they took the unusual step—as late as 1939—of issuing an official statement asserting:

'It was in relatively recent times that the exportation of the *hevea* seeds was prohibited in the state of Pará . . . a measure totally useless since none was adopted either in the State of Mato Grosso or in Bolivia where the richest rubber is grown.'*

But the fact remained that a cargo of 70,000 seeds was not going to be allowed to be shipped out of the mouth of the

---

* I am indebted to the late Robin Furneaux for drawing attention to this document in *The Amazon* (London 1969).

Amazon without—at the very least—enquiries as to its value, origin and destination, references to a higher authority and substantial delays. Wickham could afford delay as little as impoundment if he were to take full advantage of his fast ship and get the seeds to Kew Gardens before they rotted and became infertile. Somehow he had to circumvent the customs officials at Belém.

He could not avoid calling there. No ship could sail out of the Amazon without clearance, and the head of the customs was a formidable official, whom Wickham identifies in his book only as 'Baron do S-'. And Wickham had no doubt at all that the Baron—if he once guessed the extent and purpose of the cargo—would detain the ship 'under plea of instructions from Rio' if he did not place an interdiction on its departure altogether. Yet something had to be said to the Baron about the nature of the cargo: too many people had been involved in loading and stowing the plants to pretend they did not exist.

Fortunately, the British Consul at Belém—a certain Mr Green—'entered into the spirit of the thing' in Wickham's words. He agreed to accompany Wickham on his call on the Baron and that they should base their request for rapid and cursory clearance on grounds which stuck as closely to the verbal truth as they could while being totally misleading as to the substance of their statement. The holds full of seeds were represented as being a small collection of 'exceedingly delicate botanical specimens specially designated for delivery to Her Britannic Majesty's own royal gardens at Kew'. The implication was that Wickham was another Wallace with a few rare plants—orchids perhaps?—for Queen Victoria's pleasure gardens; and that the Queen was eagerly awaiting this delicate tribute from the Amazon forests. Wickham went on to explain to the baffled Baron that

'Even while doing myself the honour of thus calling on his Excellency, I had given orders to the captain of the ship to keep up steam, having ventured to trust that his Excellency would see his way to furnish me with immediate dispatch.'

Mr Consul Green nodded his corroboration and support. There was no hint of commercial quantities of seed; no mention of rubber; no suggestion that the royal *pleasance* at Kew was also the agricultural research and development centre for the whole British Empire.

The Baron was far too gentlemanly to demand an inspection of a gift for a Queen. He gave his consent to the *S. S. Amazonas* sailing out of the estuary of the Amazon. Wickham was 'now fairly away' with his illicit haul.

Once out at sea, he persuaded Captain Murray to open up the hatches and sling the crates of seeds up on lines fore and aft where they benefited from the fresh air and were safe from the rats in the hold. He got Murray to put him ashore at Le Havre, from whence he took the express channel packet to England and sped to Kew to tell Dr Hooker of his *coup*. He arrived in the middle of the night and Richard Collier in his dramatic account* tells how he threw stones at the doctor's bedroom window to wake him up and tell him of the imminent arrival of the 70,000 seeds.

Hooker also 'entered into the spirit of the thing': he turfed out the contents of the orchid house to make room for the *hevea*, and he chartered a special goods train to meet the *Amazonas* on arrival at Liverpool docks and speed the cargo southwards to Kew. He was—Wickham recorded—'not a little pleased'. A fortnight later when Wickham revisited Kew he was able to see the 'pretty sight' of tier upon tier, row upon row of his seedlings germinating in the hot-houses.

Now it was the turn of Clements Markham in the India Office to find the ultimate destination for Wickham's *hevea*.

Southern Burma was first considered, but the fall in value of

* *The River that God Forgot* (London 1968).

[55]

the rupee led to cuts in government expenditure on agricultural experiments. Ceylon was the next proposed destination, and the seedlings (by now in a more robust condition) were shipped to botanical gardens and later to plantations there. But—despite Wickham having explained that his *hevea* had flourished on relatively high ground on the banks of the Tapajós—the popular conception that the whole Amazon valley was low-lying and swampy led to planting the seedlings in unsuitably low-lying parts of Ceylon. It was not until the seedlings were eventually introduced to Malaya that perfect conditions were discovered, and what had been a wild crop on the Amazon was translated into a successful plantation crop on the diametrically opposite side of the world.

The process took several decades; indeed, almost half a century was to pass before the Brazilian rubber barons were to realize that the goose which had laid their golden eggs had taken flight on a wild migration, and that it was an English merchant adventurer who had opened the birdcage. During that half-century rubber was to dominate the life of the upper Amazon and, more particularly its tributaries. The last years of the nineteenth century were to be the age of the rubber boom and the rubber barons' extravagances: their opera house at Manaus, their wives' Parisian clothes, their Portuguese tiled houses, their Havana cigars, their laundry being sent to Europe (the Amazon water was deemed to taint the whiteness of their linen suits). It was to be many years also before the Amazonian rubber was to become a source of a scandal that would bring some parts of the region into international disrepute.

4

THE RAILROAD MEN

One of the tributaries of the Amazon that was particularly dominated by rubber in the mid-nineteenth century was the Madeira, which runs from the Bolivian border northeastwards to join the Amazon itself near Manaus, a port which already had ocean-going shipping links with North America and Europe. Not only was much rubber grown and collected along the Madeira's banks but—more importantly—it was a natural exit route for the rubber grown in the jungle interior of Bolivia. Indeed, the only other exit route for Bolivian rubber to the world's markets was the desperately lengthy westward one: by mule over the Andes to the Pacific and then by sea around Cape Horn—a journey which seldom took less than six months from the rubber tree to the factory in Philadelphia or Amsterdam or Liverpool.

The sea route round the Horn was hazardous, but not nearly so hazardous as the shorter route by river. Because although the Madeira was navigable with very little difficulty for the 600 miles between San Antonio and Manaus, the 200 miles immediately upstream of San Antonio was (and is) an almost incessant series of rapids and waterfalls. This was the stretch that joined the Madeira to the river Mamoré, which ran deep into the rubber-rich Bolivian jungles. Even the most skilful canoers or raft-handlers could not negotiate these turbulent waters, and cargoes had to be unloaded and man-handled through long stretches of swampy, fever-infested forests— with all the attendant costs and losses. The 'natural' route between Bolivia and the Atlantic was thus rendered inoperative by natural obstacles.

The first person to think seriously of a way around these obstacles was a young officer of the US Navy. Lieutenant Lardner Gibbon had explored the waterways from Vinchuta in Bolivia to the mouth of the Amazon in 1851, travelling by canoe and correcting the existing maps as he went. Already the Bolivians were beginning to think that this 2,250-mile route might be important to them if their relations with their Pacific neighbours—Peru and Chile—were to deteriorate. Gibbon made a very thorough job of his survey, and when he had the misfortune to lose his only barometer, he improvised by using a thermometer and his coffee pot to calculate altitude from boiling temperatures. When he came to the difficult 200 miles between Guajará-Merim on the Mamoré river and San Antonio on the Madeira, he counted nineteen major sets of rapids and falls. He recommended cutting a mule-track to by-pass each of the nineteen hazards, and calculated that if this were done the travelling time from La Paz in Bolivia to Baltimore in the United States would be reduced from 118 days (the fastest possible time by the Pacific/Cape Horn sea route) to 59 days. The Bolivians filed his report and nobody set about cutting a mule-track.

When the project came up for serious consideration twenty years later, America had moved into the height of the railway boom. No longer did young officers think in terms of mule-tracks or even roads: the railway seemed the answer to all modern development and communication problems. And the American officer who next examined all aspects of the problem was a very much more formidable, experienced and worldly man than Lieutenant Lardner Gibbon.

Colonel George Earl Church had been born in 1837 and at the age of twenty went to work on the railways, migrating to Argentina as a member of a topographical engineering mission on the south-west frontier of that country. Here he gained valuable experience, not only of railroads and surveying but also of cavalry warfare against the Indians of the pampas. When the American Civil War broke out in 1861 he returned to his own country and rose to command a brigade in the Army of the Potomac, later moving on to act as a war correspondent for the New York Herald in the Mexican wars of 1866–67. In later life he was to become involved in the Trans-Canada Railway and—despite his American citizenship—to be elected a Vice President of the Royal Geographical Society in London. In 1868 this remarkable man was at the very height of his energies, and it was in that year that he turned his attention to Bolivia and the problems of the Madeira and Mamoré rivers. It did not take him long to reject proposals for a canal by-passing the rapids in favour of the more fashionable concept of a railway.

Colonel Church's role was analogous to that of a modern merchant banker attempting to put together a multi-national deal in Latin America: he had to bring all the interested parties together and convince them of his own good faith and entrepreneurial capacity. The Emperor of Brazil mistrusted the Bolivian government and considered all Bolivian private companies to be shifty or incompetent, or both. But he was prepared to trust and do business with the redoubtable Colonel Church, and so by 1870 a company—the Madeira/Mamoré Railway Co.—was set up with the agreement of both countries; it was committed to start work within two years and to conclude it within seven. Little did anyone guess that it was to be more than six times that span before the railway was completed.

Church's initial problem was raising money from the banks. It was hard to raise enthusiasm for projects in Bolivia in that year: the Minister of the Interior had just been buried alive by unfriendly Indians and the resultant publicity had put people off. Undeterred, Church persisted and raised the necessary capital. But within a year work had stopped.

The English company involved had found the going too tough for them. They served a writ for voiding the contract in the chancery court in London on the grounds that it had been misrepresented to them and 'that the country was a charnel house, their men were dying off like flies, that the road ran through an inhospitable wilderness of swamp and porphyry ridges alternating, and that, with the command of all the capital in the world and half its population, it would be impossible to build the (rail) road.'

For several years the lawyers argued and work on the ground was at a standstill. Eventually the way was clear for Colonel Church to approach other contractors and start again.

This time he went to his own country—the United States—where railroad contractors were making fortunes opening up the far west and where there was confidence that no conditions could be too harsh for American technology. The firm he chose was P. & T. Collins of Philadelphia. So confident was this experienced company that they signed an even more demanding contract than their predecessors: they would start within four months and complete the project within three years. The agreed price that they would receive was to be £5,900 a mile of railroad completed. Both the company and the casual labour market in Philadelphia thought the contract represented a bonanza: 80,000 labourers applied at the offices of P. & T. Collins for jobs on the Madeira river.

But things soon started to go wrong again. No sooner had the advanced party of engineers established itself in 1878 at San Antonio (the point where the rapids begin) and erected a temporary wharf, than bad news reached them. The follow-up steamer—the S.S. *Metropolis*—from Philadelphia, with the bulk of the work force and all the supplies and wages on board, had been ship-wrecked before it even reached the mouth of the Amazon with the loss of more than eighty lives.

Those already at San Antonio now felt cut off and their rations were dwindling. Scant supplies were supplemented with monkey and parrot meat. (One Irish workman on a hunting expedition for such meats was surprised by a jaguar so close up on him that all he could do was to swing his rifle at it, shattering the butt and deterring the jaguar.) When the Americans made a start on cutting down the forest, they found that the largest trees—even when severed by axes and saws —remained upright, supported by neighbouring trees to which they were inexorably intertwined by creepers. The rate of progress was far slower than expected: in the forests of North America a team of three lumber-jacks could clear 1,500 yards of path three-foot wide in one day, but in the Amazon jungle the distance was a bare 200 yards.

Soon there was trouble with some of the workforce. The manual labourers had agreed to wages of one dollar and fifty cents per day when they signed on in the United States. Now that the full horror of the working conditions was revealed, they demanded two dollars. The most militant were the Italians. But they met their match in Mr Tom Collins (the 'T' of P. & T. Collins) who pointed out to them that they still owed the company for the cost of their transportation from Philadelphia—or elsewhere—to San Antonio until they had worked for six months (they would only be entitled to their fares home after two years' service). So far from the company paying them more, they owed the company if they stopped work. To make his point, Mr Tom cut off all rations for the striking workers and even refused to give them food in return for offers to go back to work: a day's work would come first, the rations afterwards.

This led—predictably—to open revolt among the Italian workers. More than a hundred of them refused to budge from their camp: Mr Tom responded by getting his 'loyal' workers to build a stockade of sections of steel railway line round the camp, thus converting it overnight into a veritable cage. He demanded the surrender of the strike leaders and posted armed sentries round the camp with orders to shoot attempted escapees. For good measure, he filled the signal gun of the steamer which had brought them up-river with grape shot and trained it on the camp. Mr Tom considered that the Madeira/ Mamoré railway project, in the face of all the natural hazards and deprivations involved, was the equivalent of active service; and it followed that strike action was the equivalent of mutiny in the face of the enemy.

Mutiny was soon to be followed by desertion. When eventually seventy-five of the Italian workers got out of the cage, by promising to start work again, they slipped out of the camp —without any proper rations, maps or compasses—and set off on foot through the jungle in a westerly direction aiming for Bolivia and ultimate repatriation. Not one of the seventy-five was ever seen or heard of again: Indians, jaguars, snakes and starvation must be assumed to have accounted for all of them.

Meanwhile the work of cutting a path for surveying and construction continued. The axemen complained of fire-ants which fell on their heads as they struck the trees; the surveyors complained of sweat-flies that clustered round their eyes; those attempting to escape from the insect life encountered piranhas in the river*; everyone complained of mosquitoes that struck men down with malaria; medicaments were so short that bogus quinine pills were distributed to try to keep up morale.

In such conditions, the Italians apart, morale was at best shaky. It was not unusual for the leader of a 'corps' of American workers to be given sealed orders, only to be opened after the canoe taking them to their destination had been despatched back to San Antonio, as the tasks were so onerous and dangerous that further defections were always feared if transport were available. Not only had seventy-five of the labour force taken themselves off, all the cattle imported as food had also escaped into the forests, and rations were once again short, even for the 'loyal'. The monkeys and parrots were also getting

---

* One of the American engineers, Neville Craig, lost a finger to a piranha early on; but it did not deter him from writing much the fullest and best account of the American enterprise: *Recollections of an Ill Fated Expedition* (Philadelphia 1907).

[62]

harder to bag, as—wary of the intruders—they retreated further into the jungle.

Working parties who were in camp away from the main base found it difficult to persuade their Indian support staff to go between camp and base because one of their number was thought to have been killed by a hostile tribe. The Americans were themselves disdainful of this pusillanimous attitude until a working party, which had left its own American cook behind in camp to prepare a meal for their return, got back to find him dead—shot through with three arrows. Spirits did not improve when the arrows were identified as those of the Parentintin tribe, who were reported normally to roast their victims before eating them—only saving the shin bones to be converted into flutes. The Americans had observed that all Indians—including their own support staff—moved stealthily and could approach unseen and unheard: now no man felt safe even in his own tent or when felling a tree or taking a bearing. The jungle, they felt, was not neutral but distinctly hostile.

Eventually, however, it was not the dangers and privations on the ground that brought about the collapse of the venture, but lack of finance from home. P. & T. Collins were unable to meet the wage bill because they themselves were not being paid by the Madeira/Mamoré Company. The reason for this was that the bonds which had been issued to finance the original British enterprise had been bought up by speculators, when they could be acquired cheaply at sixteen per cent of their face value; the speculators then, by dint of massive bribes and pressure, persuaded the Bolivian government to withdraw the concession granted to Colonel Church, and also brought an action claiming that (as had been declared before in the case of the first British attempt) the project was beyond the resources of the contractors. Facing financial difficulties at home, labour difficulties in the field and the intractability of the terrain, P. & T. Collins succumbed: they went bankrupt and many of their labour force were obliged to try to find their own route home.

[63]

This cleared the way to distributing the money held in trust by
the company (a sum much larger than the current market value
of the shares suggested) to the bondholders: the speculators
made a profit of over 200 per cent on their bonds.

To the bedraggled American engineers, surveyors and
labourers who were either repatriated by the company (the
lucky ones) or attempted to make their own way home by canoe
and were often left stranded on the banks of the Amazon or the
streets of Belém (the less lucky ones), the whole enterprise
must have seemed an unmitigated disaster. 221 American lives
had been lost—counting those who died of disease, were killed
by Indians or drowned at sea on the passage to the Amazon—
out of a total of 940 men sent to the region; as one of the survi-
vors (Neville Craig) pointed out, this was a casualty rate of 23 per
cent, as compared with the casualty rate in the American Civil
War which had shocked the nation by reaching 10 per cent.

But the losses had not been entirely in vain. Something had
been achieved. 320 miles of narrow track had been surveyed
and cut through the forest; a 25-mile long swath of 100-feet
wide had been cut down for the beginning of the rail line; some
30,000 cross-ties—sleepers—had been prepared; they had
even laid four miles of track and run an engine (appropriately
named the 'Colonel Church') up it regularly. Any successors
—although in 1879 it must have seemed unlikely that there
would be any successors—would find something on the
ground on which they could build.

Before, during and after P. & T. Collins' attempt to build the
railway, explorers and other travellers continued to find that
the rapids on the Madeira river above San Antonio rendered
the region beyond those rapids—on the frontiers of Bolivia
and Brazil—one of the most inaccessible and inhospitable in
the whole Amazon basin. Attracted by its very remoteness,
James Orton, an American lecturer on natural history at Vassar
College, attempted to explore the Beni river which runs

[64]

A warrior of the Xavante tribe – traditionally one of
the fiercest in the Amazon basin.

A Xavante warrior

A tribal ceremony performed by warriors of the Xingu tribe in whose territory Colonel Fawcett is widely believed to have been killed.

Colonel Fawcett, whose disappearance in Mato
Grosso has caused speculation ever since.

Rattin, the Swiss trapper who claimed to have found
Fawcett, with Consul-General Abbott.

A Xingu house in construction and life inside a hut
of the Tucano tribe.

Riverside life at Iquitos on the upper Amazon in Peru.

Cattle ranching is possible on Marajo Island at the mouth of the Amazon, but buffalo are used for meat, milk and transport in the areas which are under water for much of the year.

Buffalo on Marajo Island

Alligators abound in the Amazon swamps and are
frequently well camouflaged even when showing
their teeth (as right-centre below)

roughly parallel with the Mamoré river, but further to the west. He never completed the task: his Indian companions deserted him, and in 1877 he died while making the journey home by the westward route through Bolivia and Peru. A few years later, in 1880, Edwin Heath, another American and this time a doctor as well as an explorer, concluded the task begun by Orton: he completed tracing the route of the Beni river and established a link between it and the Mamoré—naming his new-found waterway after Orton. Heath constructed a settlement at the mouth of the Orton river, which he also named Orton, and it was to this trading station that one of the most remarkable of Anglo-Saxon lady travellers set out from England in 1896.

Lizzie Mathys had been born in London in 1870 of Swiss stock and married Fred Hessel, a commercial clerk in the City of London. They set out together to make their fortune in rubber, Hessel having been offered a job as a manager at Orton. But because the Madeira/Mamoré railway was still not completed by the time of their journey, they decided to avoid the hazards of the rapids and the endemic Yellow Fever above San Antonio and to make a very much longer river journey: they would continue westwards on the Amazon beyond the confluence with the Madeira, would pass through Iquitos and then move southwards down the Peruvian tributaries of the upper Amazon, eventually turning eastwards by the Manú and Madre de Dios rivers to end up at Orton—very close to what was to become the furthest terminal of the Madeira/Mamoré railway. This phenomenally round-about journey covered 4,000 miles of river and took Lizzie Hessel and her husband fourteen months from Belém (at the mouth of the Amazon) to their destination.

During this period they encountered hazards every bit as alarming as those on the Madeira and Mamoré rivers: fellow passengers died of fever; a launch upset drowning their closest companions; the Indians with them proved unreliable, and those not with them proved 'hostile savages'; they went without adequate food for long periods and were frequently wet,

[65]

hungry, tired, sick and frightened. But during all these trials and tribulations Lizzie continued to write gossipy social letters home*, commenting on how her dignity did not allow of her talking to second class passengers on the Amazon steamer, on how she was giving up wearing corsets, on how her pet monkeys and dogs died, on how the wives of rubber traders beat and chained up their Indian servants, on how a snake slipped out from under her long dress in the forest, on how she yearned for fashion magazines and dress patterns, and on how—when she finally arrived—she was treated as 'Queen of Orton' by European clerks and Indian servants alike. She managed to carry her own Victorian drawing-room outlook with her through every steaming swamp and violent encounter, showing that English spirit of ordered self-sufficiency which has already been remarked in Bates and Wallace.

The single most arduous passage of Lizzie Hessel's whole journey was the crossing of the so-called Isthmus of Fitzcarrald. This was a pass between the Serjali and Manú rivers (450 miles west of the Mamoré) which Lizzie traversed on foot and by mule, and where she encountered 'any amount of snakes'. Carlos Fitzcarrald** was renowned for having cleared a track and transported a river launch across the isthmus, and a romanticized film about this exploit was made by the German director Werner Herzog. He was drowned when accompanying Lizzie and her husband before they crossed his pass, and Lizzie recorded in her matter-of-fact way in one of her letters home that 'they found Mr Fitzcarrald washed up on some trees'. Indeed, if ever an argument were required for building the railway to bypass the Madeira rapids, a quick reading of Lizzie Hessel's letters, recounting the horrors of the alternative route, would provide it.

* They are delightfully edited by Tony Morrison in *Lizzie: A Victorian lady's Amazon adventure* (London 1985).
** Although Fitzcarrald was the son of an Irish-American sailor, his mother was Peruvian and he was born and brought-up in Peru as a Peruvian citizen. His story, however engaging, is therefore outside the scope of this book.

P. & T. Collins had been defeated in their task, but—
improbable as it had seemed that there would be successors to
take on the task of completing the rail line—successors there
were to be. In 1903, Bolivia was more than ever preoccupied
with its requirement to find an outlet to the Atlantic for her
rubber. On the one hand, demand had increased and prices
were high. Access to the Pacific, on the other hand, had
become even more precarious. The year in which P. & T.
Collins had given up—1879—was also the year in which the
Pacific War between Chile and a Peruvian/Bolivian alliance
had broken out. When that war came to a close in 1883, Bolivia
lost its maritime provinces altogether and, despite the
provision for a subsequent plebiscite, continued to have no
access to the ocean. The Bolivian government was therefore
prepared to pay a high price for the completion of the
Madeira/Mamoré railway, and to pay in the commodity most
readily available to them—land. By the Treaty of Petropolis in
1903 Bolivia ceded all the land known as the Territory of
Acre—a vast tract of jungle surrounding the upper reaches of
two Amazonian tributaries called the Purús and the Juruá—to
Brazil in exchange for a firm undertaking by the Brazilian
government that it would put its full financial weight behind
the railway project.

The Brazilians were as good as their word. The new railway
company had a capital of eleven million US dollars. More
importantly, the two decades since the P. & T. Collins fiasco
had seen important engineering developments, and—despite
this—the need for huge quantities of imported labour was
recognized. Workers were brought in from everywhere: the
United States, England, Ireland, Continental Europe and the
Panama Canal zone—where an even more formidable and
bedevilled project was in its final stages*. The most experi-

---

* For an account of the frustrations and difficulties of constructing the
Panama Canal, see Chapter 8 of the author's *The Quest for Captain Morgan*
(London 1983).

[67]

enced contractor in Latin America—Percival Farquhar from Pennsylvania —was put in charge of operations. Even with all these resources, the 230 miles of rail track were not completed until 1912 by which time some 30,000 workers had been treated for dysentery, typhoid and malaria and the recurring horror story about railways (be they through Red Indian country of the Wild West, the swamps of central America or the Burma of the Japanese occupation) that 'every sleeper cost a life' had already begun to circulate. Indeed, there is some evidence that on one short stretch of the line through a particularly malignant malarial swamp—the Abunã Strait—the death toll did amount to very nearly a life for every cross-tie.

The irony of the opening of the Panama Canal was that it happened within days of the outbreak of the First World War and was completely eclipsed by that event: a temporary and purely presentational set-back that did nothing to detract from the value of the canal. The irony of the completion of the Madeira/Mamoré railway was that it coincided with the beginning of the fall in the price of rubber: a permanent and fatal set-back that undermined the whole viability of the railway. Within a year or two the rubber producers of Bolivia could not afford to send their low-value product down the high-cost line. The railway that had absorbed so much effort and extracted so high a price—both in human suffering and in treasure—lay idle, or if (as the author discovered when he visited it and travelled on it for the brief ten miles between Porto Velho and San Antonio) not wholly idle then at best more like a railway museum than a vital economic link. Wickham's raiding of the rubber seeds had undermined the Bolivian and Brazilian product with Far Eastern rubber, and by doing so undermined the achievement of his fellow Anglo-Saxons: the Amazon had used one trespasser to take its revenge on others.

[68]

5

THE INVESTIGATORS

In 1907 two young American railroad engineers set off from the Pacific coast of Colombia on what was, even by the adventurous standards of the time and place, likely to be a more than usually dangerous trip. But they little knew the horrors that lay in store for them, nor the effects that these were to have on the whole subsequent life of at least one of them.

Walt Hardenburg was a 21-year-old from Illinois who had been employed variously as a labourer and surveyor since leaving the security of his father's ranch; he was a good-looking enterprising lad who aspired to find better paid and more challenging work than he had had in Colombia on the pro- jected railroad from the Madeira to the Mamoré River in the southern part of Brazilian Amazonas. He was accompanied by W. B. Perkins, a much less highly motivated youth who was greatly under the influence of Hardenburg's stronger per- sonality; he too hoped for a better job in Brazil. Both young men had spent the greater part of their savings in equipping themselves for the long journey over the Andes, and down the upper waters of various tributaries of the Amazon which would lead them eventually to their destination of Manaus.

The crossing of the Andes itself was a rare and remarkable achievement: it involved the hiring of mules and many weeks of climbing over the bare rocky mountain passes, crossing narrow valleys by precarious bridges and skirting deep ravines by cliff paths whose width was often to be measured in inches rather than feet. After seventeen days, they had crossed the water- shed and found themselves on the head-waters of the Putamayo River—here only a stream, tumbling amid boulders, but later to become one of the wide and majestic tributaries of the Amazon. It was not until they had stumbled down the banks of this torrent for some further six weeks that they had managed to buy a canoe and hire two Cioni Indians to help them paddle it on to—as they hoped—civilization. After a week of shooting rapids and coping with the foaming white waters, the Cioni said that they could go no further: they were entering territory beyond the ken of their tribe. The two Americans battled on alone.

On the way down the upper reaches of the Putamayo they encountered the usual hazards to which such travellers were exposed. Hardenburg woke one night to find a quarter-inch hole drilled in his hand and his arm engulfed in a stream of blood, following the attentions of a vampire bat. They inadvertently grounded their heavy canoe on a sandbank in mid-river, and—even after unloading all their possessions—found themselves unable to budge it. It was the end of the rainy season and the prospect faced them of weeks, if not months, of being stranded. They shot tapir and collected turtles' eggs for food, narrowly escaping the attentions of an alligator who had fancied the same clutch of eggs. Eventually, having been ignored by one party of Indians who gave them a wide berth and no offer of assistance, they were helped by a boatload of 'police' on their seventh day on the sandbank.

Indeed, this appearance of an armed band was the first indication they had had that something unusual was going on in the region. The river Putamayo, down which they were travelling, was the frontier between Colombia and Peru—but not a very formally agreed frontier. The scattered Colombian settlers, mostly independent rubber farmers, were being subjected to raids and harassment by the Peruvian rubber growers and traders, who in turn were supported by a boatload of troops sent from Iquitos. The Peruvian settlements were all part of the commercial empire of Julio César Arana, the rich, powerful and unscrupulous boss of the Peruvian Amazon Company.

When Hardenburg and Perkins put in at the first Colombian settlement they came to, all this was explained to them and they were advised to keep clear of the troubled area by arranging a portage of their canoe to the parallel Napo river which was free from such hostilities. This they set out to do.

But, despite their intentions, they could not avoid involvement. When they reached the lonely outstation where they had hoped to obtain help for the portage of their canoe and baggage between the Putamayo and Napo rivers, they heard a grisly tale. Their host—a Colombian rubber planter called David Serrano—had recently had his bungalow and plantation raided by Arana's men; they had raped and carried off his Indian wife, kidnapped his son, stolen his ship-load of rubber and left the planter with threats to return if he did not give up trying to earn a living on a stretch of river which they considered the preserve of the Peruvian Amazon Company. Hardly had Hardenburg had time to digest the implications of this horrendous story, than he heard fresh evidence of the gunlaw that prevailed on the Putamayo. The agent of the Colombian Government, who had been sent to Serrano's estate to investigate the raid and negotiate with Arana's manager that there should be no repetition of it, was himself stabbed by Arana's men; a Peruvian gunboat and sixty Peruvian troops on one of Arana's Mississippi-type river-boats appeared on the river; a major campaign to rid the river of Colombian settlers appeared to be underway. The unfortunate Hardenburg and Perkins had stumbled into the action under the auspices of the losing side and were themselves arrested and beaten up by Peruvian troops engaged in a major raid up the river on Arana's behalf.

By dint of emphasizing their American citizenship and claiming to be far more important and better connected than they were, Hardenburg and Perkins eventually regained their liberty. Hardenburg—who had demonstrated his powers of leadership increasingly as their plight had become more acute

—was allowed to roam around the Peruvian Amazon Company's base of El Encanto for some days until the company's river-boat could take him to Iquitos. Perkins agreed to stay on at El Encanto until their baggage had been retrieved and join up with Hardenburg at Iquitos. Thus might have ended a nightmarish interlude in the two men's travels and their plans might have been put together again without undue detriment to their future.

In fact, something radical had happened to Hardenburg in the few days he had spent at El Encanto—something which was to affect the rest of his life and which was to result in a major international scandal in London and Lima, which was to involve Sir Edward Grey—the British Foreign Secretary—and the House of Commons, which was to bring to prominence and knighthood Sir Roger Casement, which was to shake the stock market in the City of London, and which was to trouble the conscience of the British public as few things had done in the self-confident twilight of Edwardian England.

Hardenburg had had his eyes opened to a series of horrors much worse than the raiding of Colombian settlements by Peruvian ruffians, much worse than the beating up of American travellers, even worse than the raping and kidnapping of a planter's wife and children: he had—in his own words—had a glimpse of 'a devil's paradise'. The devilry was the grotesque treatment of the Indians who laboured on rubber estates by the overseers of the Peruvian Amazon Company. In his few days wandering around the encampment of El Encanto he found evidence of floggings and shootings, of men being put in stocks of more than medieval brutality, of the deliberate starving—often to death—of labourers, shameless exploitation of child labour and of the enforcement of young Indian children as concubines for the overseers. The atmosphere of fear, brutality and corruption at El Encanto shocked him far more deeply than any of the rough treatment to which he and Perkins had been exposed: he was convinced that he had been detained by a gang of unbridled murderers and torturers whom it was his clear duty to expose.

Hardenburg's first thought was to confront Julio César Arana with the evidence of what was being done by his employees, in the confident expectation that Arana would put a stop to such abuses. Hardenburg had a thoroughly uncomfortable and even frightening voyage to Iquitos, being chivvied, bullied and cheated by the master of Arana's river-boat. When eventually he got there, he made straight for the American honorary consul (whose main business was that of being the town's dentist) and told his story. To his surprise and consternation, the consul was unmoved by his tale; in fact, he had heard it all before and was already resigned to the fact that gunlaw and the enslaving of the Indians was practised up the Putamayo. He congratulated Hardenburg on having escaped from the region himself and strongly advised him to concentrate on retrieving his friend and his baggage and not to stick his neck out by approaching Arana. Having issued his warning, the consul returned to his dentistry.

Many other travellers, intent on finishing their journey and finding a job, would have taken the advice. Not so Hardenburg; his American conscience had been aroused and he was determined not to rest until he had righted the wrongs he had witnessed. Despairing of getting any substantive help from the consul, Hardenburg decided that he would pursue his own enquiries to build up a dossier that would command investigation and action. He obtained temporary work in Iquitos and awaited the arrival of Perkins.

When Perkins did eventually reach Iquitos, many weeks later, he was hardly recognizable: the rigours of his prolonged stay at El Encanto had not resulted in the retrieval of their baggage, but had left him haggard with under-nourishment, ill-treatment and worry. All the horrors which Hardenburg had glimpsed in his brief days of liberty at El Encanto had been testified to by Perkins' much longer stay. He had witnessed the repeated flogging of Indians of which Hardenburg had only seen the traces; he had seen with his own eyes Indians shot dead by overseers for no more crime than that of faltering with their backbreaking loads of rubber; he had had to stand by while twenty-nine 'prisoners' of the Peruvian Amazon Company were shot or hacked to death by machetes; he had seen men placed for so long in the stocks that they could never walk again; he had been present while some Huitotis Indians who had offended the company had been rounded up and burnt alive in their huts; he had seen young Indian girls captured in the forests and forced into the overseers' brothels or sold to others down river. The 'devil's paradise' which Hardenburg had diagnosed had been confirmed in every last gruesome detail.

Hardenburg persuaded Perkins to return to the United States for medical treatment (he had been suffering from malaria from the outset of their journey) but resolved to stay on himself and continue with his search for further convincing evidence with which to arouse the indignation of public opinion and—more particularly—of the shareholders of the Peruvian and other rubber companies. Soon he stumbled on a further source of evidence: a local newspaper-man was run out of town in Iquitos by Arana's agents for publishing broadsheets with complaints against the Peruvian Amazon Company's treatment of its Indian labour. Hardenburg was able to get hold of copies of the broadsheets and details of those who had supplied the information. But in the process of pursuing his enquiries Hardenburg soon attracted unwelcome attention from Arana's henchmen; the consul reiterated his warnings and told Hardenburg of a previous investigator who had been killed in a back alley of Manaus, his eyes sewn up and his ears blocked up as a warning against seeing or hearing too much.

Hardenburg was not put off his investigations, but he was deterred from confronting Arana with the evidence he had accumulated. He had a tense interview with the boss of the

Peruvian Amazon Company, whom he found immensely worldly and self-confident, but avoided disclosing either what he had heard or why he had lingered on in Iquitos. He had already learnt enough, from contacts who had supplied information to the banned newspaper and from others in the bars and saloons of Iquitos, to doubt whether Arana could be innocent of the knowledge of the fiendish regime operated in his name up the Putamayo. Hardenburg did not want to end up on the pavement of a back alley himself. So he decided to move on and pursue his enquiries first in Manaus and then—when they were completed and he had saved enough money for the transatlantic fare—to go on to England and make his revelations there.

There was a good reason for Hardenburg to choose London as the place for his disclosures. It was not only that the English had a reputation for righting wrongs the world over; there was a more specific reason. One of the facts which had most shocked Hardenburg had been the discovery that the nefarious Peruvian Amazon Company was a British-registered enterprise, with British directors, a City of London office, and its shares quoted on the London stock exchange. Even if Julio César Arana, the Peruvian boss of the Company, might be a party to the atrocities that he had witnessed, surely the English directors could not be so? Surely here he would find ready sympathy for his objectives, a public platform for his righteous indignation, and the speedy means to right the wrongs he had unearthed? It was the moment for the American investigator to hand over responsibility to the English.

Hardenburg arrived in London in July 1908 determined to find allies in his one-man struggle to put a stop to the massacres and atrocities on the Putamayo. His first thought was to approach the English directors of the Peruvian Amazon Company direct. They were a formidably reputable group. John Russell Gubbins, shortly to become acting chairman, was an old South America hand now in his sixties who had spent more than thirty years in business in Peru where he had been the friend of successive Peruvian presidents. Henry Read had a similar background, was also a director of the London Bank of Mexico and had other City interests. But the most imposing of the three English directors was Sir John Lister-Kaye, Old Etonian, Guards Officer, member of King Edward VII's Household, handsome husband of an elegant London hostess and director of innumerable other companies; he was *par excellence* a symbol of probity and fair play and his mere presence on any company board was enough to raise that company above suspicion of tawdry practices. Hardenburg —hardly surprisingly—knew none of the three. But when he discovered who they were, he thought they would be only too likely to dismiss him and his allegations as wild traveller's tales; they would have more confidence in the reports of their South American partner and co-director—Arana, with his smooth and convincing manner—than in those of an unemployed would-be railroad engineer who had been bumming around the Amazon with no very clear purpose or credentials.

So Hardenburg turned his attentions to the press. He took lodgings near Euston Station and systematically set about calling on publishers and newspaper editors, telling them of his experience and showing them his witnessed statements by Perkins and by some of the contacts he had made in Iquitos. No-one was interested; or, if they were interested, no-one was prepared to risk publishing scandalous allegations about the practices of a company registered in London which had on its board such eminent figures of Edwardian society as Sir John Lister-Kaye.

One editor however, though he had no intention of publishing the story himself, had a constructive suggestion: Hardenburg might take his evidence to the newly-founded Anti-Slavery and Aborigines Protection Society, run by the Reverend John Harris. This Hardenburg did. Harris was himself a remarkable man. He had been one of the prime movers in exposing, eight years earlier, the infamous Congo rubber scandal which had awakened the conscience of Europe to the price in human lives which was being paid for the latex exported by King Leopold of the Belgians from his private fief in Central Africa. Here at last was someone who had proved that he was not to be intimidated by fear of legal action or of offending the hierarchy. Harris was convinced of the genuine nature of Hardenburg and his cause. The Anti-Slavery Society however had no widely-read publication of its own, but it did have good links with the most celebrated medium for exposing the seamier side of Edwardian life—the well-established and highly-controversial *Truth*. The acting director of *Truth*, Sydney Paternoster, shared Harris's conviction as to the *bona fides* of Hardenburg—particularly when he discovered that the latter was not expecting payment for his revelations. *Truth* now put its own investigative team to the task of verifying and filling out Hardenburg's dossier. The Colombian consulate-general in London contributed corroborative material; and the British honorary consul in Iquitos, who was contacted while on leave in Wales, confessed to having frequently heard similar accusations, and even to having passed them on to the Foreign Office. The editors of *Truth* were convinced that they had enough solid material to launch one of their most spectacular campaigns.

On 22 September 1909 *Truth* blazened across its columns an article entitled 'The Devil's Paradise: A British-owned Congo'. Below were printed all the lurid particulars of Hardenburg's and Perkins' reports: of how a slave empire had been set up in the Amazon basin, of how men were starved and flogged, of how children were murdered for sport, of how women were forced into harems for licentious overseers, how run-away workers were fed to the guard dogs. The revelations were appalling . . . and more were promised in subsequent editions.

The reactions of the Peruvian Amazon Company were

curious. A journalist who was sent to interview the directors at the London Wall offices of the company met the Peruvian representatives of the company, not the English directors. The Peruvians did not so much deny the charges as attempt to discredit their sources. And this they did with surprising verve and verisimilitude. Hardenburg, the reporter was told, had demanded £7,000, with menaces, from the company's legal adviser in Iquitos; he had attempted to sell to a Manaus newspaper for extortionate prices material designed to damage Julio César Arana, and when he had failed he had doctored a bill of exchange in his favour to the tune of over £800. He was a blackmailer and a forger: his testimony was valueless and criminally inspired.

When the same reporter went back a few days later to pursue the story with the company, having published a guarded version (omitting Hardenburg's name) of what he had been told, he again was unable to meet the English directors but this time met an official of the company who offered him a bribe—a plain envelope containing a large bank note. They had misjudged both the reporter and his newspaper—the *Morning Leader*—which retaliated to this attempt to buy its silence by publishing a series of headlines on 27 September reading 'Our Congo . . . Strange Story of Banknote . . . Peruvian Amazon Company and the *Morning Leader*', and below them a full account of the bribery attempt. Not all the defamation of Hardenburg could retrieve the damage done by this fatal blunder.

But the defamatory charges were awkward because they were the well-documented product of a long-standing and consistent attempt by Arana to compromise Hardenburg. Ever since Arana had first suspected in Iquitos that Hardenburg was enquiring rather too closely into conditions on the Putamayo, he had been laying traps for him: first he had persuaded his lawyer, who happened to be a pupil of Hardenburg's (the latter had been eking out his existence by giving English lessons) to

[78]

spy on Hardenburg and manufacture charges against him. Then he had persuaded the editor of *Amazonas*, a Manaus daily which had links with his company, to prefabricate a circumstantially detailed tale of offers and menaces. Finally he set up a worthless crook called Muriedas to ingratiate himself with Hardenburg during the latter's stay in Manaus and to persuade Hardenburg to cash a forged banker's draft on his behalf while the latter purported to be too ill to go to the bank. The net had been carefully constructed: Hardenburg could not deny his acquaintance with the Iquitos lawyer, nor with Muriedas, nor his connection with the doctored draft (though he could—and did—deny ever having met the editor of *Amazonas*).

The slanderous charges did not discredit Hardenburg with the Anti-Slavery Society, nor with *Truth*, nor with his friends, nor even with the subsequent investigators of his charges; but they did serve Arana's immediate objective of discrediting him with the British directors of the Peruvian Amazon Company; Arana was able to show them privately the 'evidence' which he had collected, without risk that this would be subjected to questioning in the courts, and he found Messrs. Gubbins and Read and Sir John Lister-Kaye all too ready and anxious to believe that the charges against their company were the malicious fabrications of a blackmailer.

But however much Arana might reassure them, the British directors could not stifle their unease. The campaign in *Truth* went on, week after week, throughout the autumn of 1909; letters from *Amazonas* fuelled the campaign with fresh facts; shareholders of the company became worried and restive at the annual general meeting. More serious still, the Foreign Office was beginning to take an interest in events up the Putamayo; it had requested a report from the only independent British traveller who had recently visited the region—a Captain Whiffen on prolonged sick-leave from the 14th Hussars. Whiffen was an enthusiastic anthropologist and it was this interest which took him—despite being unfit for more normal service—up the Amazon and the Putamayo. Whiffen's report had not been reassuring: although he had had the impression that much 'cleaning up' had gone on, he had still seen and heard enough—whipping of Indian girls, dismantled stocks, reports of men being beaten to death—to give credence to Hardenburg's reports.

Thus goaded, the British directors decided that they ought —however belatedly—to send out a commission of enquiry. They were confident it would silence their critics and vindicate Arana, and they took good care to ensure that it was composed of reliable people: Colonel the Hon. Reginald Bertie, a personal friend of Sir John Lister-Kaye, was to head the commission for a fee from the company of £2,500; and Henry Gielgud, an accountant employed by the company who had already absolved the company's employees from misconduct in a previous report, was to be its secretary—with an increased salary, also of £2,500. Even Arana, who had understandably been against any enquiry, was confident that this one would not unduly embarrass him.

Then, on 21 July 1910, the whole picture changed. Sir Edward Grey, the British Foreign Secretary, insisted on the attachment to the commission of the British Consul-General in Rio de Janeiro—Mr Roger Casement. That there was to be an independent government official on the enquiry was—from the company's point of view—bad enough; that it was to be Casement was far worse. He it was who had first exposed the Congo rubber scandal and alerted the Anti-Slavery Society several years before when he had been Consul in Leopoldville. He had a reputation for getting to the heart of the matter where atrocities were concerned, and he would not be amenable to inducements or threats.

The ostensible reason for his appointment to the commission was—from Arana's point of view—ironic. The dreaded overseers on many of Arana's plantations were young

Barbadans—often no more than children—imported and armed to prevent escapes or mutinies among the Indian labour force. Barbados was a British Colony and so the young overseers were British subjects. This provided grounds for Sir Edward Grey to claim the requirement for official involvement.

Casement was 46 at the time of his appointment to the Putamayo commission and his career in the Consular Service had been an erratic one. He had made his name over the Congo affair some six years earlier, but his cantankerous temperament, his propensity to feel slighted by more elegant superiors, his romantic Irish moodiness . . . these characteristics all combined to make him a difficult colleague to fit in to a traditionally minded and close-knit branch of the public service. Like Richard Burton—another member of the Consular Service in Brazil almost half a century earlier—he was an 'odd-ball': unclubbable, unpredictable, unbiddable.

After his name and fame had been established by his bold revelations of King Leopold of the Belgians' misgovernment of the Congo Free State, Casement had been lionized in London society and appointed a Companion of the Order of St Michael and St George—CMG—at an unusually early age. He felt that the Foreign Office owed him preferment to a senior consular post to his own liking. Lisbon disappointed him, and he retired to Ireland on rather unconvincing sick leave; Santos, the sea port for São Paulo in Brazil, to which he was subsequently appointed, appalled him and he grumbled unceasingly; Pará, the Brazilian port at the mouth of the Amazon where he was next sent, struck him as 'hideously expensive . . . perfectly awful'; and even when he was promoted to the highly desirable post of Consul-General in Rio de Janeiro he immediately set about complaining to the Foreign Office that his predecessor had over-charged him for the office furniture. Had his superiors known that, in addition to these tiresome quirks, Casement was a committed Irish Nationalist and an insatiable practising homosexual, even his public reputation and his fearless intellect would not have saved him. But they did not know, and to Sir Edward Grey he seemed the ideal man to put some teeth into the Putamayo commission.

Casement had been recalled to England for briefing and sailed from there direct to the mouth of the Amazon, where he met the other members of the commission—including Bertie and Gielgud—and set out by steamer to Manaus (only stopping en route at Otacoatiarra long enough to quarrel with the customs officials). Manaus was enough for Colonel Bertie: he collapsed and returned sick to England. The others pushed on up river as far as Iquitos, complaining bitterly of mosquitoes, flies, putrid smells from the river and lack of baths on the steamer. At Iquitos both the Prefect and the French Consul, while suggesting that there was nothing to fuss about on the Putamayo, left Casement with the impression that—although they might not themselves be shocked—conditions there were none-the-less shocking. Questioning of Barbadians who had been employed as overseers by the Peruvian Amazon Company made matters sound even worse.

The commission now decided—it was already September 1910—to go on by launch to the controversial region itself. They did their best to insulate themselves against the rigours and boredoms of the terrain: cases of whisky were loaded on board, and evening bridge sessions—for surprisingly high stakes—were instituted. They sailed slowly along the Igaraparana and Putamayo rivers, stopping at all the rubber-collecting stations; observing evidence and taking statements. It was grim work. Scores of Indians displayed savage weals on their buttocks; statements were taken relating murders, mutilations and tortures; cases of burning Indians alive and of shooting stragglers were all-too-well-documented; cases of rape and wanton sadism were almost routine. Casement reckoned that the Indian population had been reduced owing to these enormities by two-thirds over the period of a few years, and that within a decade they would be wiped out altogether unless the Company's practices were halted. The argument, which had so frequently been put forward in the company's offices in the City of London and in Iquitos, that the reports of killings must be untrue because 'the Indians were the goose that laid the golden egg—rubber', was unconvincing when the totally self-interested and short-term nature of the Putamayo operations was revealed: no man thought beyond his own immediate financial and sexual gratification.

The cramped, hot, insect-ridden voyage of the commission was made all the more unbearable by the company of the white managers and overseers who received them and entertained them at the settlements. One manager organized a dance by a thousand Indians—almost all of whose naked bodies displayed signs of the violence inflicted on them—in apparent unawareness of the effect this spectacle produced on his guests. Some white managers spoke openly of the crimes they had committed, apparently assuming that their hearers shared the view that the Indians were not to be considered as human beings having any personal rights. These same managers attached themselves to the commission, travelled on their launch, and shared their meals; indeed, if Casement and his companions were to be able to visit the settlements they had to do so under these repellent auspices.

Casement himself managed to quarrel with most people, including Gielgud (whose offence was to address him as 'Casement' and not as 'Consul-General'). More seriously, as was to be later revealed in very extraordinary circumstances, he behaved in a surreptitiously debauched way with a large number of the Indians and others with whom he came in contact. For while Casement was making notes of all the evidence of atrocities that he and the commission were able to detect, he was also keeping a 'black diary' of his own homosexual relations with those to whom he successfully made advances along the route. And there were surprisingly many of them. It could be argued that this—however distasteful—was his own affair. But in one important sense it was not: had Casement's proclivities and practices been discovered, they would inevitably have undermined the credibility and authority of his report with those whose belief and respect it was essential to maintain—Sir Edward Grey, the Foreign Office, the House of Commons, the American and Peruvian Governments and (most important of all) public opinion in Edwardian England. Casement it seems was prepared to jeopardize his whole work by his philandering, and when it is considered how Arana might have exploited such information (Arana's attempt to *manufacture* similar but much less potent slurs on one of his other accusers was to emerge shortly) the real nature of the risk to his report—as well as to his reputation—appears. But for the moment his extramural activities remained not only undetected but unsuspected.*

Indeed Casement did not wait until the commission had completed its work before making a preliminary report to Sir Edward Grey. On 7 January 1911, having come home specially for the purpose ahead of the other members of the commission, he informed the Foreign Secretary that 'the condition of things fully warrants the worst charges brought against the agents of the Peruvian Amazon Company'. In May of the same

* Casement's 'black diaries' only came to light when his papers were seized six years later (in the middle of the First World War) after he had been arrested, on charges of treason, for attempting to raise a revolt in Ireland with German help. After he had been sentenced to death at the Old Bailey in London, copies of the diaries were reportedly shown to a number of influential people to dissuade them from campaigning to save Casement's life. The British Home Office have always declined to release the diaries or explain what happened, but many accounts have been published, notably René MacColl's *Roger Casement* (London 1956). One theory put forward by Casement's supporters is that the diaries, although in his handwriting, were in fact copies he had made of the diaries of one of the most notorious sadists on the Putamayo river; this theory is not generally held to be convincing.

year, Grey sent the British directors copies of Casement's full report and later the same month his Parliamentary Under-Secretary at the Foreign Office revealed the broad outline of its contents to Parliament. There was a stir, but hardly as yet an uproar.

Sir Edward Grey was himself a man of the highest liberal principles. He had played a major role in obliging King Leopold to make over his estates in the Congo to the Belgian State after the revelation of the abuses and atrocities there, and he was as determined as anyone—as Hardenburg himself —that now that the Putamayo atrocities had been confirmed they should be ended. He immediately put in hand—through the British Minister in Lima and the British Ambassador in Washington—pressure on the Peruvian Government to stamp out the abuses and arrest and bring to trial the villains. As a result of his pressure, a gun-boat had been sent from Iquitos up the Putamayo with a judge carrying more than two hundred arrest warrants. He recommended a knighthood for Casement, and—as Sir Roger—the latter returned to the Putamayo to check on the progress of arrests, only to find that most of the culprits had been tipped off and allowed to escape. Casement was received by President Taft in Washington and together they discussed ways of obliging the Peruvian government to be more effective in righting the wrongs. One way seemed likely to be the most effective: to publish Casement's horrifying report—with all its grisly details—in full. Such a revelation would shame the Peruvian government into action. So it was that in July 1912, more than a year after Casement's report had been submitted and more than four years after Hardenburg had first stumbled on the truth of conditions up the Putamayo, the whole story came into the public domain.

There were immediate repercussions. The Pope urged his bishops in South America to be mindful of protecting the Indians and set up Mission Stations. The Duke of Norfolk set up a fund in London to provide for an Indian sanctuary. A canon of Westminster Abbey preached a hard-hitting sermon against the British directors of the Peruvian Amazon Company —naming them from the pulpit. The German rubber industry declared a boycott against Putamayo rubber. The Peruvians themselves set up an Indian Protection Service. The company's shares slumped. And then on 5 November 1912 the final step was taken: the Speaker of the House of Commons in London issued a search warrant authorizing the impounding of the company's records for perusal by a special committee of the House empowered to summon whatever witnesses they wanted and to examine the British involvement in the atrocities.

The hearings of the Committee of the House of Commons were prolonged and conducted under the rigorous searchlight of publicity. Not only did the committee itself include a number of prominent Parliamentary figures such as William Joynson-Hicks (a future Home Secretary), Lord Alexander Thynne and John Swift MacNeill KC (renowned for his pugnacious cross-examinations both in Parliament and the law courts); but the witnesses also briefed prominent legal figures to defend them: even among the junior Counsel were Raymond Asquith (the Prime Minister's son) and Douglas Hogg (a future Lord Chancellor). The stage was well-lit and the actors were anxious to shine. Casement and others went through the evidence that had already been made public, amplifying it with photographs and sombre exhibits.

The first really tough cross-examination was that of the unfortunate Gielgud, whose blinkered and anodyne report from his first visit as accountant to the Putamayo had done so much to lull the company and the Foreign Office into inactivity and acceptance of Arana's reassurances. Had he not thought £7000-worth of rifles was an odd item on the balance sheet of a rubber company, asked Lord Alexander Thynne? No, said Gielgud, there were jaguars about in the Amazon forests. If he had managed to visit the forest region and remain unaware of all the talk of atrocities, was he not 'a little financial babe in the wood', MacNeill asked Gielgud. 'If you like that description, I will accept it' was all that Gielgud could reply. No, he had not seen 'the mark of Arana' on the flogged Indians, because perhaps 'they were in a part of the body that one does not usually look at', and when the Indians went through the forests without clothes they naturally got rather scratched. Gielgud was recalled for even rougher treatment later: why had he suppressed the item in his original notes 'gastos de conquistación—£11,400'? Did not this expression translate into English as 'costs of conquest'? Had he not himself described it elsewhere in his notes as 'expenditure incurred in reducing the Indians to subjection'? If, as he maintained, the word 'conquistación' meant 'recruitment', why did that rendering not appear in the House of Commons dictionary? Were not the expenses really the cost of rifles? Did he not realize that 'reducing the Indians to subjection' had been effected by brutality and murder? Gielgud finally left the witness stand looking either callously dishonest or almost unbelievably naive.

Next it was the turn of the luckless Gubbins. No, he said, he had not read the articles of association of the company—although he was acting chairman—so he had not thought it odd that these explicitly forbade shareholders to enquire too deeply into the way the company ran its affairs. No, he had no idea what the rubber tappers were paid. No, he was not surprised that there was no provision in the company's accounts for feeding the Indians as 'in the rivers there are an immense abundance of fish'. No, he had not noticed a payment to a section chief for hunting fugitive Indians. No, he had not thought it necessary to go out to see conditions for himself. No, he would not have been able to hold on to his lucrative appointment if he had offended Arana. No, he was not aware that during the nine months when the company had resisted

Foreign Office pressure for an enquiry a further twenty-five murders had been committed by its employees.

The other British directors fared no better on the witness stand. Sir John Lister-Kaye, it transpired, had no knowledge either of the country, or of the conditions, or of the trade in which the company was engaged, 'he did not know the language in which the proceedings of the Board, of which he was a member, were frequently conducted.' One and all they left the House looking—at best—like foolish and negligent old men.

The court-room tension of the House of Commons committee rooms was soon to rise even higher. Two key witnesses voluntarily crossed the Atlantic to appear and give evidence. One was Julio César Arana, the other was Walter Hardenburg. At first the Peruvian's sophistication, poise and authoritative manner impressed both his questioners and the spectators; Arana was not the common ruffian that all had expected. But as the relentless questioning proceeded, first his patience, then his dignity and finally his temper cracked. Arana was revealed for what he was: arrogant, truculent, devious, inconsistent and unconvincing. Hardenburg, on the other hand, was unshakeable under cross-examination. Gradually the whole process by which Arana had attempted to blacken Hardenburg's reputation—with his charges of forgery and blackmail and even implication of perversion—was exposed. The Peruvian's connections with the originators of the blackmail charges and with the spurious nature of the forged bond were uncovered; it even became clear that Arana had persuaded a Manaus hotelier to put Hardenburg and Muriedas (the actual forger of the bond) in a single-bedded hotel room and later to aver that they had spent the night in conditions of 'intimacy'. A further, and even more elaborate, attempt to brand Captain Whiffen —the originator of the subsequent report on the Putamayo which had worried the Foreign Office—as another blackmailer fell to the ground when Whiffen himself explained Arana's attempts to get him drunk and to write an incriminating note in a language he did not understand.

Despite Douglas Hogg's advocacy, Arana emerged at the end of the committee's hearings as the unscrupulous exploiter and tormentor of the Putamayo Indians which he was. Their final report to the House of Commons declared that he 'had knowledge of and was responsible for the atrocities'.

The British directors of the company were in a tight spot: although the crimes committed were all on the Putamayo and would thus normally have been outside the jurisdiction of the English courts, the foreign crimes which could be brought to book at home included those committed under the Slave Trade Acts. Thus if the directors had connived in the hunting down of slave labour they would have to stand trial. The Committee found that 'evidence of a system of forced labour appears in the company's papers'; but it went on to conclude that there was 'no evidence that the British directors made themselves individually parties to any overt act which would expose them to a charge under the Slave Trade Acts'. So far so good. But the report then went on to a damning indictment of 'the culpable negligence of the British directors': they had 'assumed positions to which are inseparably attached responsibilities they failed to discharge . . . and their conduct . . . is deserving of severe censure.' The committee found that the two directors with South American experience must have had reason to suspect the attitudes and practices towards the Indians—at least to the point where they should have set in hand their own enquiries. As for Sir John Lister-Kaye, who had known so little about anything, he was censured for 'taking a directorship under conditions so humiliating, and for allowing his name to be used as an inducement to attract investors into a company of whose business and proceedings he knew nothing at all.' All of them ought to have realized the responsibility of being pioneers of commerce in a new and uncivilized region. Indeed, the report thundered, 'they should not lightly have exposed to risk the good name of England'—grave censure indeed at any time, but perhaps especially in the high noon of the British empire.

But the Anglo-Saxon role had been principally a positive one throughout the sad chapter of events. The appalling state of affairs on the Putamayo might have—almost certainly would have—gone on much longer had it not been for the up-river journeys of the American Walter Hardenburg and the Anglo-Irishman Roger Casement: a grim chapter in the story of Anglo/American involvement with the Amazon had reached a satisfactory ending after nearly five years of struggle.

6

THE ADVENTURER

By 1914, Theodore Roosevelt had already achieved more in his fifty-six years of activity than half-a-dozen more normal American public figures. He had combated corruption in New York as its police commissioner; he had established an international reputation as a big-game hunter; he had raised a regiment of Rough Riders to fight in Cuba; he had been elected governor of New York state; as Vice President he had inherited the Presidency of the United States when his predecessor was assassinated; he had been elected President in his own right; he had inspired and masterminded the construction of the Panama Canal; he had won the Nobel Peace Prize for his intervention in the Russo–Japanese War; and he had written some half-dozen popular books. But his quest for excitement had not yet been satiated. As a former President, with time on his hands, he was looking for the ultimate adventure. The Amazon was to provide it.

Roosevelt was—among other things—an ornithologist of some celebrity* and before setting out on a lecture tour of South America he persuaded the American Museum of Natural History that they wanted specimens of flora and fauna from the banks of the southern affluents of the Amazon. He gathered a small group of travelling companions to go with him on what he declared was to be 'not intended as a hunting trip, but as a scientific expedition'. The two principal companions

---

* In 1910, while on a formal visit to England, he had found time to spend a day bird-watching in the New Forest with Sir Edward Grey, the British Foreign Secretary.

were to be his son Kermit and George Cherrie. Kermit Roosevelt was a young engineer who had, only two months previously, broken two ribs, lost two teeth and seriously injured his knee when a derrick on which he had been working collapsed; but Kermit was declared by his father to be 'practically all right again' and firmly recruited. Cherrie, who was recommended by the Museum authorities, was another tough character who had knocked around South America as an ornithologist and had found nothing odd about combining his bird-watching with fairly active gun running. Roosevelt later was to write of Cherrie that he 'willy-nilly had been forced to vary his career by taking part in insurrections . . . twice he had been behind bars in consequence, on one occasion spending three months in prison in a certain South American State, expecting each day to be taken out and shot'. The ex-President was putting together a pretext and a team for his adventure but as yet had no very clear idea of what that adventure was to be.

It was the Brazilian Foreign Minister who came up with the idea for which Roosevelt had been waiting. At a lunch in Roosevelt's honour in Rio de Janeiro he told him of a river in Western Mato Grosso whose headwaters had been discovered some months before by Colonel Rondon, the head of the Brazilian telegraph service and the foremost Brazilian explorer of his time. Rondon was convinced that his unknown waterway would prove to be 'a very big river, utterly unknown to geographers' and that it probably flowed into the Amazon. He had named it the Rio da Dúvida—river of doubt. It would be a hazardous but worthwile venture to attempt to go down the river by canoes to determine its destination—every whit as intriguing a prospect as going up a known river to determine its source. Rondon himself was prepared to accompany the ex-President, and the Foreign Minister offered logistical support from the Brazilian government. Roosevelt decided he need look no further for an objective: 'I eagerly and gladly accepted' he wrote in his subsequent account of the expedition.*

The journey to the headwaters of the Rio da Dúvida was in itself a considerable undertaking. The first stage was completed in comfort and style: the President of Paraguay put his gun-boat-yacht at Colonel Roosevelt's disposal to take him up the Paraguay river to the point where he would start his overland trek. This involved riding through the swamps of the Pantanal in southern Mato Grosso and the scrub country of central Brazil. However firmly Roosevelt might have declared that his was a scientific and not a sporting expedition, he could not resist the opportunity to hunt the game that presented itself. Piles of dead tapir, peccary, bush deer, alligators and even jaguar marked the ex-President's progress through the heart of Brazil, and his book is lavishly illustrated with photographs of himself posing beside each and every species. The little Springfield rifle—'my favourite . . . with which I have killed most kinds of African game, from lion and elephant down'—was seldom idle for long.

On 3 February 1914 Roosevelt, who had linked up with Rondon and taken a considerable liking to him, set out on the final stage of their journey to the headwaters of the Rio da Dúvida: they travelled as a mule-train across the *sertão*, or scrub lands of the interior, until on 24 February they reached a camp within striking distance of their embarkation point on the Rio da Dúvida. Here the party sorted itself out.

The team who were to accompany Roosevelt consisted of his son Kermit and their fellow American Cherrie, and also Colonel Rondon with two Brazilian compatriots one of whom was a doctor. The six explorers were supported by sixteen paddlers for the seven canoes, five of which were reasonably sound but two of which leaked and were lashed together to

---

* Published in 1914 in the United States as *The Great Adventure* and in England as *Through the Brazilian Wilderness*.

form a baggage raft. Provisions for about fifty days were embarked, but these were not full rations as Roosevelt and Rondon reckoned that they would be able to live in part off the country, since between them they had a formidable array of firearms (which was to lead to trouble). The three Americans planned to share one tent, the three Brazilians another; there did not appear to be tents for the paddlers who could be assumed to be used to sleeping in the open. They also took hammocks for everyone except Roosevelt who preferred to sleep in a folding cot, which was not immune to ants and termites and so became a considerable liability. Roosevelt lists in an appendix to his book a note on equipment and clothing: his own preferred dress was knickerbockers with long stockings and leggings over hob-nailed boots. Like all good explorers they took plenty of serious reading matter: Roosevelt's travelling library included some volumes of Gibbon, the plays of Sophocles, More's *Utopia*, Marcus Aurelius and Epictetus. He also had a writing table and camp chair, and—so that his writing should not be distracted by insect life—wore a helmet with a pendent mosquito net and gauntlets. Before long most of this carefully selected equipment was to be perforce abandoned.

From the very beginning the canoes were to give trouble. They were immensely heavy dug-outs, and Roosevelt was soon regretting that he did not have more manoeuvrable Canadian birch-bark canoes or American canvas and metal ones. Roosevelt's canoe usually started out last and ended up the day's run well ahead of the others, because Kermit (in the front canoe) and Rondon (in the second) were engaged on the time-consuming task of surveying—putting up markers and taking bearings and measurements. One of the main objectives was in this way accurately to map the course of the river as 'no civilized man, no white man'—Roosevelt recorded—'had ever gone down or up this river or seen the country through which we were passing'.

At first the going was good. The canoes made some fifteen miles a day down a river some hundred yards wide. Cherrie shot birds as specimens and monkeys as food. A diversion was caused by the discovery of a coral snake in the camp one night which Roosevelt recorded he promptly put his foot on; while Cherrie recorded in his account* of the trip that Roosevelt had danced a lively hornpipe round the snake in the general agitation. Ants also attacked them, and Roosevelt records his amusement at the doctor's underclothes being devoured, while Cherrie has a similar story about Roosevelt's. So far everything was much as expected: some excitements and discomforts but nothing perturbing.

Soon however things were to start going wrong. 'We heard the roar of rapids ahead'—Roosevelt's phrase is in the classic tradition. The hundred-yard-wide river was soon reduced to a 'rushing torrent' less than two yards across. Now that a lengthy portage was required the heavy weight of the dug-out canoes was more than ever regretted; it was necessary to cut some 200 six-foot logs and place them along the route under the canoes as rollers. The paddlers—who had insisted on being paid seven times the normal rate to accompany any expedition in which that legendary seeker-after-danger Rondon was in-volved—were harnessed to drag the cumbersome craft for several miles past the rapids. Two and a half days were lost and considerable damage inflicted on the canoes. On relaunching the canoes one of them sunk and was with difficulty salvaged. It was a mild foretaste of the difficulties that lay ahead.

From then on, there were recurrent rapids and portages. More serious was the set-back of one of the two leaking canoes filling with water at night and dragging the other one—to which it was lashed—down with it. Both broke up—being 'riven assunder' in Roosevelt's phrase—and all the gear and

* *Dark Trails* published by Putnams in 1930 in New York and London. All quotations from Cherrie are from this autobiography unless otherwise stated.

provisions loaded onto them were lost. It took a further three days to fell and hollow-out a large tree to make a replacement canoe. Then, after two days of relatively fast progress—about twelve miles a day—a worse disaster struck.

Kermit, in the leading canoe as usual, kept going in the channel too close to another series of rapids and was sucked into a whirlpool, whisked over the rapids in a canoe rapidly filling with water, sucked into another whirlpool, and overturned. One of the two native paddlers with him in the canoe managed to clamber on to the upturned canoe with Kermit but was then swept off and never seen again, while the other and Kermit managed with extreme difficulty to reach the bank in a totally exhausted and bruised state. Kermit had lost his rifle, and very nearly his life. His father commented wryly that Kermit was being a great help to him on the trip and he would not have relished the task of explaining his death to his mother and his fiancée.

Nor did the incident help relations between Colonel Rondon and the Americans; the former implied in his own account of the trip that the accident could have been avoided if Kermit had obeyed his order to bring the leading canoe in to the bank as soon as the dangerous nature of the 'furious bubblings' was realized. Indeed the surviving paddler told Rondon that Kermit had ignored not only this instruction but the paddlers' own advice and had 'insisted on his purpose' of keeping going, with fatal results. Although Rondon subsequently deplored this 'most rash' behaviour, he does not appear to have remonstrated with Kermit nor held it against him. Meanwhile they erected a sign with an inscription reading 'In these Rapids died poor Simplicio', and passed on.

Morale was not improved by two unfortunate incidents that followed almost immediately afterwards. The first was the loss of yet another canoe: when being towed through rapids the new and heavy dug-out, that had been so laboriously constructed and launched only four days before, broke loose and

A Xingu mother

A rubber tapper's house
on the Rio Negro

Peter Fleming and Evelyn Waugh (right), the two literary travellers who in the 1930s exploded many of the myths about the Amazon basin.

Wildlife of the Amazon: a puma, 'lion of the Andes' (above) and a jaguar (below)

Robin Hanbury-Tenison (above) who traversed the Amazon basin from east to west by jeep, and from north to south alone by dinghy, seen here in his jungle hammock; and Richard Mason (below) who was ambushed and killed by Indians near the Iriri river, seen here shaving in the mirror of his jeep on Bananal Island.

The headwaters of the Amazon in the Peruvian Andes.

Map of South America, engraved in 1562, shows extent of Spanish exploration along the coasts and river valleys. The Amazon is given common serpentine form; vignette above words *Gigantum Regio* shows belief in Patagonian giants.

The author at one of the sources of the Amazon in
the Peruvian Andes

sank. This left the party with only four canoes in all, at least two less than they needed to transport the whole party. Stopping to cut down more trees and hollow out more canoes made no sense when there was every reason to think that more rapids lay immediately ahead, which would involve further laborious portages.

From now on some of the party would travel along the bank on foot. On 16 March Colonel Rondon was scouting ahead in this way to attempt to find out anything he could about the future course of the river, accompanied by one of the expedition's three dogs. Dogs are always vulnerable in jungle: they suffer terribly from leeches and insects, and they attract predators. Rondon was therefore probably not very surprised when Lobo (as the unfortunate canine was called) uttered a squeal of pain; however, a few seconds later the dog gave out a further howl and staggered towards Rondon to drop dead pierced by two long Indian arrows. Rondon thought he heard voices, though it could have been the cry of spider-monkeys, and fired off his rifle to scare away the presumably hostile natives. On second thoughts he returned to the place where Lobo was shot and left some beads to encourage the Indians to think he was friendly. It was little wonder that Cherrie wrote in his journal that 'it behooved us to move with caution', and that Roosevelt wrote in his 'it behoved us to go warily'. From now on sentries were posted, and indeed this is the only communal duty which the ex-President seems to have shared.*

The immediate problem was trying to squeeze as much as possible into the remaining canoes. Several of the paddlers had fever or feet swollen from insect bites, which was hardly surprising as they did not wear shoes or boots in the forest. When they, the Brazilian doctor and the baggage had been loaded into the four frail craft, there was only room left for

---

* Apart from washing his fellow American's underwear on one single occasion, which aroused simpering comments in Cherrie's journal.

Colonel Roosevelt. Indeed even to get this priority human cargo on board a great deal of the gear and equipment had to be abandoned. From now on Roosevelt's cot was placed at night under the small emergency tent and the five other explorers slept under the one 'fly sheet'. Thus two tents could be abandoned, as were most of the surveying instruments and a good deal of personal baggage. The thirteen more mobile members of the expedition now had to make their way as best they could on foot, and since there was no path along the river it was not always easy to keep close to it.

After several further rapids had been negotiated by the river party and some Indian trails found along the bank to facilitate the progress of the rest, morale picked up a little. To consolidate the more cheerful mood, Rondon christened a sizeable affluent of the Rio da Dúvida which they had just encountered 'Rio Kermit', and went on to inform Colonel Roosevelt that the main river itself was 'by directive of the Brazilian government' to be named hereafter 'Rio Roosevelt' after him. Colonel Roosevelt was delighted, and proposed three cheers in rapid succession for everything he could think of: Brazil, Colonel Rondon, Lieutenant Lyra (one of Rondon's officers), the doctor, and even the paddlers. 'Then,' in his own words, 'Lyra said that everything had been cheered except for Cherrie; and so we all gave three cheers for Cherrie.' This was—after all—how Anglo-Saxons were expected to behave *in extremis* on the Amazon.

And *in extremis* they very quickly became. The following day although they avoided the mistake which they had made when constructing the earlier canoe—choosing a wood so heavy that it lacked all buoyancy and therefore sank—they this time chose a rotten tree to fell and it collapsed prematurely bringing down with it a number of other trees in the middle of the camp 'overthrowing everything'. Roosevelt commented that it would never have happened with northern lumberjacks. Ants again invaded the tents and this time 'ate things we could ill spare'.

To make matters worse they found that some of the paddlers —they called them *camaradas*—had been stealing the emergency food supplies: fifteen boxes had disappeared, which suggests a great deal of surreptitious eating by the culprits. Meanwhile the remaining provisions were running low and the six explorers kept themselves down to half rations, while the *camaradas* stoked up on palm shoots and the flesh of an occasional monkey, river fish or parrot. Roosevelt commented that in the American west the game supply was more abundant and wholesome.

By now, instead of flattening out, the river seemed to be getting ever more rocky, fast and perilous. For several days it was unusual for the canoe party to be able to progress for more than a quarter of an hour on calm water before the next rapids hove in sight or hearing. Worse still, they could see through the overhanging trees that there were hills ahead, and hills meant even more frequent and more difficult portages. The last few days of March were spent negotiating the worst obstacle they had yet encountered: the river ran through a gorge which had such steep sides that it was both difficult and perilous to lower the remaining canoes through on ropes. Only Kermit's bridge-building experience enabled him to rig up the necessary ropes and pulleys to achieve a task which they at first thought would be completely beyond them. Meanwhile all the luggage had to be humped over heavily-forested hill-tops because the ledges along the steep-sided ravine were too precipitous to be used by men carrying loaded packs. Even further reductions had to be made to the party's equipment, and at this stage Colonel Roosevelt abandoned his separate tent, his books, his spare shoes—indeed almost everything except his spare spectacles, a spare pair of drawers, his cartridges, and of course the famous cot, head-net and gauntlets.

Having recollected the party and its remaining chattels at the lower end of the gorge, Colonel Roosevelt took stock of the situation:

'During (the past) month we had come only about 110 kilometres, and had descended nearly 150 metres. We had lost four of the canoes with which we had started, and one other which we had built, and the life of one man; and the life of a dog which by its death had, in all probability, saved the life of Colonel Rondon. In a straight line northward, toward our supposed destination, we had not made more than a mile and a quarter a day.'

In fact, it is clear from Cherrie's account that Colonel Roosevelt was even more depressed and in much worse condition than his own account concedes. By this stage he had been ill intermittently for some weeks: in addition to a recurrent fever (which the other Americans also suffered from), he was weakened by dysentery, and a wound—which he had sustained on his leg when wrestling with one of the canoes in the water—had become infected. His heart was also giving him trouble, so that he frequently collapsed and urged the others to go on without him. When Rondon—back from one of his reconnaissances—reported that yet further ravines and perilous portages lay ahead and went on to say 'we shall have to abandon our canoes and every man fight for himself through the forest', it was too much for Roosevelt altogether. He retired to his cot in a delirious condition from which he rallied to urge—once again—the others to go on without him: 'Boys, I realize that some of us are not going to finish this journey: Cherrie, I want you and Kermit to go on. You can get out. I will stop here'.* It was almost two years to the day since another Anglo-Saxon explorer—Captain Oates of the Inniskilling Dragoons—had said to his companions in Antarctica 'I shall be gone for some time' and had walked out of their tent to meet his death in a blizzard rather than allow his frost-bitten feet to hamper their chances of reaching safety. Roosevelt's plight

* Quoted verbatim in Cherrie's book.

—though bad—was not yet so desperate as Oates's: by the next morning there was no more talk of dropping out, and no more talk by Rondon of splitting up the party. Indeed Kermit and Cherrie had been quick to point out to him that to have split up at that stage would almost certainly have been to condemn most of them to perish in the forests. It is hard to think that the doughty Rondon ever seriously contemplated anything so irresponsible.

But one member of the expedition was to be left to perish alone—slowly and horribly. No one but himself could be blamed. Julio was the only one of the *camaradas* of pure European—Portuguese—extraction. He had been anxious to sign on as one of the paddlers, but had proved a liability from the start—shirking his work, grumbling, whining for favours and latterly filching the rations of his fellows. Things had come to a head when the chief of the *camaradas* had caught him red-handed stealing food and had punched him in the face. Julio had harboured a grievance, 'borrowed' a rifle, waylaid the chief on a path between two camps and shot him dead at close range. Rondon was far ahead of the party when the incident happened—on another of his reconnaissances—and it was left to Roosevelt and the doctor to pursue Julio in case he should run amok and murder any more members of the expedition. They soon found he had abandoned his rifle in his flight, and decided that there was no point in pursuing a man who could do them no further harm and whom they would have to arrest and keep under close guard—an almost impossible task in the straitened circumstances they were now in. Roosevelt decided to abandon Julio to his fate and when, three days later as they were paddling down the river, they saw the unhappy man pleading on the bank to be allowed to surrender to them they did not relent. However, Colonel Rondon, who was by then with the main party once more, was not happy with this and after consulting Roosevelt later in the day, decided that, as the Brazilian officer responsible for the whole party, he ought to send two men back to apprehend Julio after all. Although they searched hard, they failed to find him.

Like the incident which had led to the drowning of Simplicio, this affair also might have led to a more serious rift between Rondon and the Americans had not both sides shown some consideration of the other's point of view. Rondon did not take his decision to send a party back for Julio without explaining his action first to Roosevelt, and Roosevelt deferred to Rondon's right to deal as he saw fit with the men he had recruited. But both were shocked by the attitude of the other: Roosevelt felt that Rondon would have put an undue burden on the other members of the expedition by retrieving and taking along with them 'an individual who had excluded himself by his wicked instinct', while Rondon felt that to abandon voluntarily anyone in the jungle was a betrayal of 'the duty of a Brazilian officer and of a man'. It was in many ways a relief to them both that Julio was never refound.

By now three of the *camaradas* had become fatal casualties, and Roosevelt reports at this stage in his narrative that there were fears about the lives of some of the others who were the worst affected by fever. (He does not refer to the fears about himself.) The seemingly endless series of rapids continued day after day. Easter Sunday was one such typical day: they only ran a clear course down the river for ten minutes in all, and spent some eight hours in carrying the remaining equipment and provisions past rapids down which the empty canoes were run on a line.

But after Easter the worst seemed to be behind them. The river at last flattened out and runs of fifteen or even thirty kilometres a day were being recorded. On 13 April they camped 'for the first time for several weeks' out of earshot of rapids. And the hunting and fishing became easier: big *piraiba* fish and numerous piranhas were caught and consumed; Cherrie shot three meaty monkeys, and a brace of *jacú-tinga* birds—like small turkeys—was bagged. The party was no longer starving.

Then on 15 April they found a board on a post by the bank of the river on which had been carved the initials 'J.A.': clearly some rubber man, more adventurous than his fellows, had penetrated this far *up* the river. Habitation could not be too far ahead. Further on they came to an empty hut in a clearing. Another hour's paddling brought them to the first human they had seen since they set out on the river seven weeks earlier: an old black rubber tapper gave them a friendly greeting. From now on they were travelling on a relatively smooth waterway which was known to connect with civilization.

For Colonel Roosevelt, it was only just in time. His fever was recurring ever more frequently and his leg had now developed such a serious ulcer that he was unable to walk. An awning was stretched over the central section of the most stable canoe and he was laid out there and paddled onwards. Had there been further gorges and chasms to contend with, it is difficult to see how he could have negotiated them; and further hunger and worry about the outcome might have aggravated the fever to a fatal extent. As it was he commented:

'It is not ideal for a sick man to spend the hottest hours of the day stretched on the boxes in the bottom of a small open dug-out, under the well-nigh intolerable heat of the torrid sun of the mid-tropics . . . but I could not be sufficiently grateful for the chance'.

Where there were further rapids, there was also help in the form of extra hands, local expertise and well defined and cleared paths for the portages. Eventually it became clear that the Rio Roosevelt was known in its lower reaches to the rubber men as the Rio Castanho but—much to Roosevelt's gratification—this name did not appear on any maps. Eventually the Castanho formed the Aripuanan and both flowed into the

Madeira which in turn flowed into the Amazon. As the party continued their progress, conditions became steadily easier: the final lap was completed by steamer to Manaus.

The nature of the discovery they had made had been substantial. Previous maps had not only not indicated their river, but had suggested contours which made its very existence impossible. Cherrie had assembled a valuable ornithological collection. Roosevelt summarized the whole achievement in only slightly exaggerated form when he wrote:

> 'We put upon the map a river some fifteen hundred kilometres in length, of which the upper course was not merely utterly unknown to, but unguessed at by, anybody; while the lower course, although known for years to a few rubber-men, was utterly unknown to cartographers. It is the chief affluent of the Madeira, which is itself the chief affluent of the Amazon.'

But, quite apart from the incidents of the drowning of Simplicio and of the retrieving or not of Julio, the whole American involvement in the enterprise had probably put more strain on Rondon than the Americans realized at the time. When the latter came to give his lectures about the trip, in Rio de Janeiro the following year, there were hints at some of these stresses and strains. Early on, Rondon despaired of Roosevelt's daily excursions into the forest with his gun ever producing any game for the pot, on account of his shortsightedness and his very audible progress through the undergrowth. Roosevelt's restless impatience to keep moving, particularly in the early stages before his health collapsed, had meant that Rondon had to conduct a much more rapid and less thorough survey of the river than he would have wished; indeed, he complained of not being able to put some of the technical equipment he had brought to proper use because of the continual urge to press on. On the other hand, it must have sorely strained Rondon's patience when he had to waste a whole day—at a later and more crucial stage—to send a party back for Kermit's dog, because its owner had forgotten to embark it in his canoe in the morning. Also, one gets a much clearer picture from Rondon's lectures than one does from Cherrie's or Roosevelt's own account of the continual worry which Roosevelt's health was to Rondon; there are endless references to the ex-President's breathlessness when obliged to climb any slope, to the feared erysipelas in his leg, to his repeated fevers and how at times 'he was scarcely able to stand'. But—apart from his one unfortunate outburst about all splitting up and going their own ways (which is not mentioned in his own account)—Rondon remained calm and good-natured in the face of his eccentric companions.

Within months of Roosevelt's return home, the First World War broke out. When the United States entered the war, Roosevelt characteristically volunteered not only to go himself to fight in France but to raise a force to take with him, as he had done to Cuba. The American government declined the offer, to the fury of Roosevelt who declared that it seemed to be 'a damned exclusive war'.* But the powers-that-be were probably right in thinking that the over-weight ex-President was no longer a fit man; the Amazon adventure—with its fevers, infections and exhaustions—had permanently impaired his health, and in January 1919 he died unexpectedly at the age of 60.

The whole episode of the Rio da Dúvida had been a curious one. The Brazilian government in their commendable anxiety to draw attention to the work of discovery that—largely through the labours of Rondon—they were achieving in their own interior, took a considerable risk in proposing to a middle-aged, world-famous statesman that he should disappear into

---

* Roosevelt's four sons including Kermit, however, did fight in the war; one of them being killed.

their most unknown and perilous region. Very possibly the Brazilian Foreign Minister who proposed this particular trip to Roosevelt had little idea of what was involved, but even so, the ex-President's urge for an Amazonian adventure could almost certainly have been channelled into less genuinely dangerous paths. Had he died or disappeared, as he all too nearly did, there would have been no little embarrassment in Rio. Equally, Roosevelt himself seems to have given little real thought to the implications of his participating in such a venture. He cheerfully wrote in his book that

'No man has any business to go on such a trip as ours unless he will refuse to jeopardize the welfare of his associates by any delay caused by a weakness or ailment of his. It is his duty to go forward, if necessary on all fours, until he drops.'

But he must have known, for all his stout-hearted intentions to go on until he dropped, and for all his offers to his companions to leave him behind, that he would not in the event be left and that he might well become a liability to the others. The old trooper was gambling with other lives as well as his own. All one can say is that his companions did not grudge him his final fling: Cherrie ends his autobiography by saying 'When I recall companions I have had, good, bad, and indifferent, Theodore Roosevelt stands apart.' And Rondon—whatever his former reservations—concluded his lecture on the expedition at the Phenix Theatre in Rio by paying tribute to him as 'a man of firm, resolute and imperative character, an honest and most noble soul.'

Not all Colonels were to be as lucky as Roosevelt and Rondon. In the very same year another Anglo-Saxon Colonel was girding himself up for his own final fling into Mato Grosso and was only delayed in departing by the outbreak of the war; and this Colonel was not to emerge alive from the Amazon forests.

7

THE SEEKER FOR EL DORADO

Almost the only quality which Colonel Percy Fawcett shared with Colonel Theodore Roosevelt was mental and physical toughness. In most other respects they had little in common: while Roosevelt was an American of wide international renown and interests, Fawcett was an Englishman little known even in his own country; while Roosevelt was a newcomer to the South American jungle, Fawcett had spent many years before the First World War in delineating national boundaries in Amazonas; while Roosevelt was forever shooting anything that moved, Fawcett deplored unnecessary slaughter of wild animals; while Roosevelt came to the Amazon for adventure for its own sake, Fawcett had a very clear vision of a specific objective —and a very exciting one it was.

Colonel Fawcett had been commissioned in the Royal Artillery in 1886 and had learnt military surveying while serving in Ceylon. He was a tall, robustly built man who had been both an amateur boxer of distinction and a county cricketer. He volunteered in 1906 for special service in South America as a surveyor on loan to the Bolivian government, who were concerned about suspected encroachments from Brazil and Peru into their rubber-rich forests. Colonel Fawcett liked the country and liked the work, in which he was encouraged by the Royal Geographical Society in London. He made repeated survey expeditions between 1906 and the outbreak of the First World War in 1914. In fact, while Hardenburg was canoeing down the Putamayo—to the north of him—and Roosevelt was descending the river that was to bear his name—to the east of him—Fawcett, unknown to either of them, was trudging through the rain forests along the Bolivian-Brazilian frontier. He interrupted his labours to return to Europe and fight in France during the war, distinguishing himself by winning the DSO for gallantry in the trenches.

But as soon as the war was over, he returned to South America and started planning more explorations. By now he was no longer involved in frontier demarcation on behalf of others but was committed to a personal and romantic quest of his own. Fawcett had for many years been aware of the insistent and recurring reports of a lost city of antiquity in the heart of the Amazon forests. Indians of different tribes from different regions believed and repeated accounts of an ancient civilization and of a city of golden monuments—an El Dorado in the heart of the jungle. Such fables had been current since the days of Sir Walter Raleigh, but more recently a manuscript document had been unearthed in Rio de Janeiro which seemed to add authenticity to all the rumours and legends.

The document related how a *bandeirante*—a Portuguese soldier of fortune—had been searching for lost silver mines in the interior in 1753 and had stumbled, with his companions, on a mountain range gleaming with rock crystal which dazzled the explorers. At first the range seemed impenetrable, but while one of the band was out hunting for the pot he put up a white stag and—in the course of pursuing it—was led into a defile through the mountains. The next day the rest of the band followed up this lead and found themselves, after three hours' climbing, on top of a pass from which they could see, on a plain some miles in front of them, what appeared to be a European citadel. They sent out scouts cautiously, who returned reporting that the settlement was uninhabited. So the next day the whole band descended and entered the lost city. What they found was as evocatively romantic as the crystal mountains and the white stag. First they passed under 'three great arches, so high that none could read the inscriptions on them' and then passed down a broad street into a city square dominated by a black stone column bearing a statue of a man pointing with his arm to the north. Other obelisks, columns and statues lay around. But—apart from swarms of sinister black bats—there was no sign of life. The *bandeirante* and his companions followed a river out of the deserted city for three days until they came to 'cataracts . . . deep cuttings and frightful excavations'. These they assumed were mines and they endeavoured to descend them, but their ropes were too short; they had to satisfy themselves with collecting silver nails and gold coins near the supposed mines, and panning gold from the river itself. Further down-stream still they spied two white men in a canoe who declined to respond to their hails and disappeared. The expedition then pressed on to the River Paraguassu from where they sent a written report of all that they had seen to the Viceroy in Bahia.

It was this report, which had lain gathering dust in the state archives for generations, that so inspired Colonel Fawcett. In particular, he was struck by the fact that many of the details of the lost city which the *bandeirante* described tallied closely with the characteristics of other ancient civilizations, some not discovered by 1753 and all of them certainly unknown to uneducated Portuguese adventurers: the great blocks of stone fitting together with mortarless joints of almost incredible accuracy, the cyclopean structures, the carefully copied hieroglyphics . . . all these gave verisimilitude to the account.

The 1753 manuscript was reinforced by other reports, some of them very convincing, of the existence of lost cities in the heart of Mato Grosso; the British Consul at Rio—an eminently sober-minded man by the name of Colonel Beare —declared that he had himself been taken to a ruined city in the jungle which also boasted statues and black stone columns, but unfortunately he had had to return to the coast without managing to take any proper bearings. There were scraps of pottery and inscriptions which came to light from time to time to fuel the theory that there had been an advanced civilization

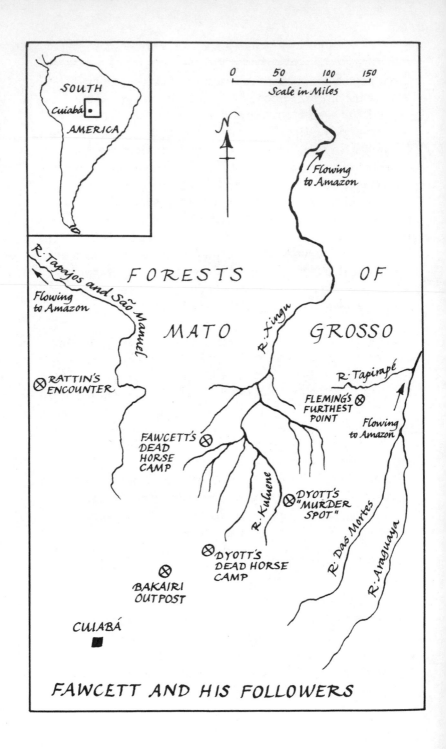

FAWCETT AND HIS FOLLOWERS

of some sort in the region in antiquity. Even more encouraging to Fawcett was the discovery—resulting from intensive exploration based on no more solid evidence than his own—of ancient Inca cities in the Andes; Hiram Bingham of Harvard had, as recently as 1911, stumbled on an overgrown flight of rock steps climbing through jungle into the mountains which had led him to the hitherto unlocated site of Machu Pichu. What could happen a few hundred miles to the West, could surely happen in the even-less-known fastnesses of Mato Grosso.

Not everyone was convinced of the straight-forwardness of Fawcett's motives. His own surviving son, Brian, was given to hinting at the 'politically explosive' nature of his quest. Colonel Rondon, now a General and the nationally revered authority on the Indians, was always somewhat hostile to Fawcett's enterprises and was thought to believe that he was in the pay of one of the big oil companies and was, in fact, prospecting: why else should he be so secretive about his movements, and so vague about the routes he had covered? Others, aware of the spiritualist element in Fawcett's mental makeup, which he shared with his contemporary Sir Arthur Conan Doyle, thought that his explorations had some more metaphysical content; such speculators about his objectives also noted his scientific bent (he had patented the Ichtoid Curve) and putting the two strands together decided that he was looking for some source of unknown energy in the forests of the Amazon; there were theories that earlier civilizations had extracted energy from the sun, that strange towers had been constructed in this connection, and even that the lost city of Atlantis had been destroyed by an explosion resulting from storing such energy. Fawcett's last message, as we shall see, was thought by many to have been deliberately misleading about his whereabouts: so the mystery about his fate was to be extended to a—probably unnecessary—mystery about his motives.

Fawcett had seldom been lucky with his companions. Before

the First World War, when he had been surveying on the Bolivian frontier, he had enjoyed the support for a while of two admirable NCOs from the Rifle Brigade called Costin and Leigh; and in 1911 he was joined by another useful Englishman called Manley who had worked for him earlier in Devonshire. Even then, there had been less happy companions, like the Englishman recruited in La Paz who lost his false teeth in a river and had to be sent home before he starved in consequence. But after the war, when he changed from surveying to pure exploration, he had a succession of disasters as companions. There was 'Butch' Reilly, an Australian whom Fawcett described as:

'six feet five in height and broad as a barn door, claimed to be a major and a V.C., a broncobuster, a sailor and several other things. "And what's more", he said, "you can't teach me anything about a horse . . ." A man like Butch should be well able to stand up to forest travel, and I engaged him gladly.'

Disillusionment was to come fast. When the moment for the expedition to move off arrived, he fell off twice while trying to mount, declaring that 'these ain't horses like I know them', and then fell off four more times even though the horses never moved out of a walk. Three days out, Butch collapsed altogether and had to be sent back.

Fawcett's other companion on that occasion, a young man called Felipe, also had frailties. He was terrified of wasps. He shot Fawcett's favourite dog to stop it chewing the saddlery. He let his horse get drowned. He took to lying on the ground, moaning and declaring he could go no further. Finally he developed what Fawcett described as 'a sort of got-it-all-over disease'. Fawcett on that occasion, as on so many others, was forced to turn back owing to the inadequacy of his companion.

But one has some sympathy for Felipe and the others who tried to keep up with Fawcett. The latter had a way of attracting danger and discomfort. His own book* reveals that he or his acquaintances were always encountering the most extreme manifestations of the Amazon's horrors: one man was strangled by a boa-constrictor while sleeping in his hammock; another man hung on to the edge of a canoe as it was towed to the bank of a river and was then found to have been 'eaten from the waist downwards' by piranhas; a third man felt a tap on his shoulder while drinking at a river and turned round to find a bushmaster snake staring him in the face. Poor Felipe: all he complained about were the wasps!

The expedition on which Fawcett set out on 20 April 1925 was, from the beginning, likely to be the most demanding that even he had ever undertaken. He started from Cuiabá and appears to have planned to strike northeast through the states of Mato Grosso and Goias, across the river systems of three of the largest southern tributaries of the Amazon—the Xingu, the Araguaya and Tocantins; he would then go on to the San Francisco river (which also runs north but is not a tributary of the Amazon) and follow this to the coast. He reckoned that the journey would take him at least eighteen months and possibly much longer.

Although Fawcett planned to cross these major rivers and their own innumerable lesser tributaries, he did not plan—like Roosevelt and most earlier explorers had done—to follow the course of any river. Rather he would plunge across jungle and savannah country never previously penetrated. This scheme had three particular hazards which were additional to those experienced by river travellers: firstly, he would be able to carry very little baggage—only in fact what he and his companions would be able to carry on their backs as there would be no canoes and pack animals could not be expected to survive the terrain; secondly, he would be liable to suffer from thirst as there might

* *Exploration Fawcett* edited by Colonel Fawcett's younger son Brian (London 1953).

be long stretches out of reach of any fresh water; and thirdly, he would be continually moving from one tribal area to another and would thus be more likely to encounter hostile Indians than if he were consistently moving down a single river where there would probably be some continuity or at least some relationship between the Indians on its banks.

At the time he set off on this quite exceptionally perilous and demanding expedition, Fawcett was already 57—older even than Roosevelt had been on the Rio da Dúvida. It might have been thought that he would have selected experienced and hardened companions; but he did not. Instead he took with him only his son Jack—a newcomer to such adventures—and a friend of his son called Raleigh Rimmell. At least they seemed better prospects than Butch Reilly and Felipe.

They set out with a dozen animals—horses and mules—which obliged them to move very slowly. On the fourth day out of Cuiabá they got lost: Colonel Fawcett had gone on ahead and the others took a wrong fork in the failing evening light and had to camp without him. Raleigh Rimmel was already showing ominous signs of cracking up: he 'gloomed all the way to the Rio Cuyaba'* and opted out of the heavy work involved in river-crossing because of his bad foot. They pressed on to the settlement at Bakairi where eight very wild and naked Xingu Indians turned up in the hope of trading barter goods. On 18 May, Jack Fawcett was still writing home about the undiscovered waterfalls and rock-paintings they expected to reach within three weeks' trek from Bakairi: the whole adventure was living up to his expectations as he celebrated his twenty-second birthday. But Raleigh Rimmell's other foot had now swollen up; when he took his sock off to bathe, the skin came

---

* This remark and other information in this paragraph is based on Jack Fawcett's letters home—quoted by Brian Fawcett in his Epilogue to *Exploration Fawcett*.

off with it, and it started to swell. They none-the-less pressed on.

Finally, on 29 May, Colonel Fawcett reached Dead Horse Camp—the spot where his horse had died on the gruelling journey he made in 1920. He decided that from here on they would be entering the territory of fiercer Indians and that his *peons*—the native bearers—had better be sent back with four of the animals and the last letters home. Fawcett himself was suffering a bit from insect bites as was Jack whom he reported to be otherwise 'well and fit'. But he declared that he was anxious about Rimmell whose leg continued to give trouble but who wouldn't go back. Be that as it might, his letter to his wife ended with the words 'You need have no fear of failure'.

The most interesting thing about this letter were the co-ordinates which Fawcett gave for Dead Horse Camp: 'Latitude 11°43' South and 54°35' West.' This was also the bearing he had given for this camp in his outline of his projected trip. There can be little doubt that the camp he reached *was* the one where his horse had died in 1920, because he writes of finding its white bones. But the time between Fawcett's last letter from Bakairi, dated 20 May, and his final letter from Dead Horse Camp, dated 29 May, was incredibly short to have covered a distance of nearly 150 miles through scrub, forest and some swamp, with at least one of the party ailing. For this reason most subsequent enquiries into Fawcett's fate have concluded that he deliberately gave misleading co-ordinates to put off possible followers. He was—the argument goes—convinced that he was on to the trail of his lost city and wanted the glory to be all his own.

For the moment, nobody expressed particular surprise. Nor was there any special anxiety when no more news arrived: after all, he had always said he would be away for at least eighteen months and maybe for longer. Besides, he had no means of sending messages back now that he had dismissed the last of his *peons*. Indeed when Fawcett had returned prematurely on earlier expeditions it had usually been because of the collapse of his companions and the consequent failure of his mission. On this, his last expedition, no news and no early return might well mean that he had at last discovered his ancient civilization, his lost cities, his El Dorado. But as months stretched into years, these hopes receded.

Fawcett had never wanted rescue operations to look for him. He himself said this was because he did not want others to risk their lives on his account; his detractors said this was because he did not want others stumbling on the secrets of his discoveries. In reality he probably reckoned that rescue parties would either be too soon—that like Livingstone he would be 'found' when he had never considered himself lost; or that they would be too late—that like Stoddart and Conolly at Bokhara he would be dead before his rescuers arrived.

But by 1928—three years after Fawcett's last message had been received—anxiety and speculation had reached a pitch at which an American press syndicate thought that it would be a profitable venture to finance a search party, equipped with photographers and radio operators, to penetrate Mato Grosso and send back news stories. An experienced American explorer—Commander George Dyott—was invited to lead the party. Dyott was determined not to disappear without trace himself, and as a precaution against this he assembled a sizeable expedition. As well as two photographers and two radio men, he had more than twenty other supporters and seventy-five pack animals to carry the equipment. Clearly progress was going to be cumbersome, but Dyott felt there was safety in numbers.

Soon after setting out from Cuiabá, Dyott's party reached the tiny settlement of Bakairi, the last place where Fawcett and his companions had been incontrovertibly seen (Rimmell had been observed to be already limping even by that stage) and indeed the last 'place' they seem to have passed through at all. Here Dyott met up with an Indian called Bernadino who had teeth like tusks and who claimed to have guided Fawcett through the first stages of his journey. Bernadino offered—for a price—to do the same for Dyott. He pointed out curious blazes on trees which, he suggested, were made by Fawcett; and eventually he led Dyott to the Kuliseu river on which, he claimed, Fawcett had requisitioned for his own use two Indian canoes. At this point Dyott sent back his suffering animals; the heat had been so great that the bullocks had, in any case, only been able to travel at night. He also halted to build five more canoes, to add to the four canoes and the rubber boat which had been humped this far on the backs of the nocturnally-moving bullocks.

Dyott's water-borne party now paddled down-stream—that is northwards—to an Anauqua Indian village where Bernadino said he had left Fawcett. Dyott now felt he was hot on the trail. He had a long series of sign-language conversations with the Anauqua chief—one Aloique—and saw various chattels in the village which he took as hard evidence that Fawcett had passed this way and had left them behind: a tin trunk, and a brass trinket with the make of a London firm stamped on it. (Brian Fawcett was later to say that the trunk had almost certainly been used on a previous expedition, not on Fawcett's last one.) Aloique claimed not only to remember the Englishmen well, but to have accompanied them overland into the territory of the neighbouring tribe to the east—the Kalapolo Indians. This tribe also claimed to remember Fawcett and said that he had stayed with them and then moved on eastwards; they even went so far as to say that they had recalled seeing the smoke from his camp fires for four days after he left them—a curious statement in view of the extreme difficulty of seeing smoke rising from thickly wooded country, and the likelihood that if Fawcett had found the terrain less than thickly wooded he would have travelled too far in four days for them to have seen his smoke anyway.

Beyond the Kalapolo Indians was the land of the more

[117]

warlike Suya tribe. Neither the Anauqua nor the Kalapolo had been prepared to accompany Fawcett into such dangerous territory; nor were they prepared to accompany Dyott. They all blamed the Suya for the murder of Fawcett; although Dyott tended to think that the surly and disagreeable Anauqua chief Aloique—in whose village the trunk and trinkets had been found—was himself the culprit.

Dyott had split his party: before going overland into Kalapolo country, he had sent the porters and paddlers down the Kuliseu river in the new canoes to wait for him at the confluence of the Kuliseu and the Kuluene rivers. Now that he was on the Kuluene river, in what he imagined were Fawcett's footsteps, he felt apprehensive about pressing on further into hostile country with a depleted force. He therefore halted his overland journey eastwards and instead followed the Kuluene river down to its junction with the Kuliseu and his *rendez-vous* with his support personnel.

From the point of view of gaining further information about Fawcett, this turned out to have been an unfortunate decision; because when he reached the river junction he found that his party were importuned and molested by ever increasing numbers of Indians who gathered round them at their camp, arriving in canoes from every direction and demanding more gifts than the explorers had to offer. The scene was getting ugly. Dyott was already convinced that Fawcett and his companions had perished in these parts at the hands of greedy Indians; he did not intend to suffer the same fate. So he slipped down river, with all his party, on what he described in his subsequent book* as 'a midnight escape' and reached the wider waters of the Xingu river. The circumstantial evidence that Fawcett had been murdered somewhere beyond the Kuluene river seemed impressive, but short of totally convincing—particularly in the absence of a body.

* *Man hunting in the Jungle* (New York 1930).

The missing body—or rather skeleton—did not appear until 1950. By that date the celebrated Brazilian anthropologist and authority on the Indians—Orlando Villas Boas—had spent almost a year living with the Kalapolo tribe: he was their friend and he was trusted by them. They confided in him, after receiving assurances that there would be no retribution after the twenty-five year time gap, that they had killed the three missing Englishmen. They had, of course, ever since Dyott's visit in 1928, been aware of the details of the party and of the interest in the subject; so a certain amount of romanticizing may have been indulged in. However that might be, their story to Villas Boas was broadly as follows.

Fawcett had arrived from the west with two younger men and accompanied by the chief of a neighbouring tribe, which they did not describe as the Anauqua, but which clearly could have been. This much had been adumbrated at the time of Dyott's expedition. But now the Kalapolo went back on their —always rather improbable—story about seeing the smoke of Fawcett's camp for four days after he left marching eastwards, and 'confessed' that he had angered their tribe. They maintained that he had struck two of them in the face: one—a grown man—after a quarrel about the carcass of a duck which Fawcett had shot, and the other—a child—after the latter had been pestering him. The statements seem surprising in view of Fawcett's long and well-established patience with the Indians on all his previous expeditions. There was also mention to Villas Boas of dissatisfaction at the distribution of largesse and suspicions that Fawcett and his companions were intending to move on with the bulk of their barter goods intact (which would hardly have been surprising since Fawcett expected to be travelling through Indian country for at least a further year); so cupidity as well as anger was hinted at. At all events, the Kalapolo told Villas Boas that their chief had authorized the killing of the strangers. This had been effected by clubbing them to death in a sudden and treacherous attack by three young tribesmen who were purporting to be their guides. The bodies had been thrown into an alligator-infested lagoon and later fished out and buried to cover their traces. The Kalapolo took Villas Boas to the spot and invited him to disinter the bones; this he did—convinced that finally the Fawcett mystery was solved once and for all.

But it was not. After the bones had been repatriated to England, and restored to the family in the somewhat improbable surroundings of Claridge's Hotel in London, they were sent for analysis to the Royal Anthropological Institute. Here they were found—conclusively and indisputably—*not* to be those of Fawcett, or his son, or Raleigh Rimmell: they were the incomplete skeleton of a much shorter man than any of the Englishmen, the teeth bore no resemblance to Fawcett's, and the skull and framework left little doubt that the skeleton was that of an Amazonian Indian. So how much of the rest of the Kalapolo story could be believed? Possibly most of it; but possibly also very little or none, since self-dramatization cannot necessarily be considered a monopoly of civilized societies.

Brian Fawcett, the surviving son of the Colonel, had never accepted Dyott's findings and, when summoned to London to receive a set of bones which he was convinced were not those of his father, his brother Jack or Raleigh Rimmell (and which he irreverently christened 'George') he became even more sceptical. He did not share the general veneration for Orlando Villas Boas, but he accepted the offer of a free passage to Brazil from a Brazilian newspaper magnate and was duly flown up to the Kuluene river to meet the Kalapolo, who were so adamant about claiming to have murdered his father, to form his own opinion in the light of the evidence.

The trip was not a success from the point of view of its sponsors or of Villas Boas. Brian Fawcett remained unconvinced by the Indians' own account. He could not accept that his father would have insulted and struck them, still less that (as reputed in some accounts) his brother had been making advances to the chief's wife. He thought it odd that the Kalapolo should have said they used clubs to kill his father, as this was not their preferred weapon; and even odder that they should have buried him, when popular superstition normally forbade this. He was convinced that Villas Boas was rehearsing the Indians with their lines, under cover of participating in a 'sacred rest' from which Brian Fawcett was excluded. He claimed that Villas Boas at one moment told him not to reveal his identity, and at the next announced it to the whole tribe. When he reminded Villas Boas of the shortness of 'George's' leg bones, compared to the height of all Colonel Fawcett's party, he says that Villas Boas replied 'but perhaps your father may have had a long body and little short legs': a remark which prompted Brian Fawcett to retort that his father was not a dachshund. When one of the Kalapolo recalled the Colonel —who had been bald by 1925—as looking as hairy as Brian, the latter's doubts were further confirmed. Brian Fawcett concluded: 'the whole story was exploded, and with it had disintegrated all the so-called evidence of previous reports that the Fawcett party had met its fate here.'

Between Dyott's expedition in 1928 and the dénouement of the bones in 1950, there had been many other incompatible theories advanced. But one of these carried—and carries —particular plausibility if not conviction.

In 1932, Stefano Rattin, a trapper of Swiss origin who had for many years made a meagre living in the interior of Mato Grosso, turned up at the Frigorifico Anglo at Barretos in the north of São Paulo state. He said that for the previous five months he had been travelling south from the heart of Mato Grosso, and he had a curious tale to tell to the British man-ager at the British-owned *frigorifico* (or slaughterhouse). The tale so impressed the manager and his colleagues that he promptly wrote to his own general manager in São Paulo city saying:

'Today, we are sending to São Paulo a man who has turned up claiming that he knows the place where Colonel Fawcett is kept a prisoner by the Indians. This man has had a severe questioning by the Englishmen at the plant and although he may be a colossal liar, we have decided to club up to give him his fare to São Paulo so that he can put his tale before the British Consul . . . He claims that he has a personal message to Major Pagett, in fact, his answers to all our many questions would leave one to believe that he really has seen and talked with Colonel Fawcett, who he says he saw alive about October 18th 1931.'

The British Consul-General, Mr Arthur Abbott, was as impressed as the slaughterhouse manager; and his being so is more significant because he had known Fawcett well and even accompanied him briefly on one of his trips. Abbott took a full statement from Rattin, and a very strange one it was. In the headwaters of the Tapajos river, Rattin had come across an Indian village where an old white man, tall and bearded and dressed in skins, was being kept prisoner. The Indians had apparently been annoyed at Rattin spotting him, but—during a later bout of drinking by the Indians—the white man managed to approach Rattin and, speaking in English, said he was an English Colonel and he wanted Rattin to report his plight to the British Consul. He also sent a message to a person variously described as 'farmer Paget' or 'Major Paget'. When Rattin undertook to deliver these messages, he shook his hand and said he was 'a gentleman'. In doing so, he revealed that the backs of his hands were badly scarred and Rattin gave him some iodine, which the Indians promptly took off to paint themselves with. The white man spoke of his son 'sleeping' and wept at the recollection of this. (Brian Fawcett later found 'both the remark and the emotion utterly unlike my father'.) No attempt was made to prevent Rattin leaving the Indian village.

In his report to his ambassador—Sir William Seeds—in

Rio de Janeiro, Abbott enlarged on his impressions. To start with, he was impressed that Rattin did not want any payment beyond some reimbursement of out-of-pocket expenses involved in delivering Fawcett's message. Abbott immediately identified Paget as a former ('farmer'?) ambassador to Brazil —Sir Ralph Paget—who had been a close friend of Fawcett's; he went on

'and this is why I feel sure there is something in his story, although Fawcett's expedition was well-known everywhere, very few persons outside his intimate friends knew of the interest which Paget took in his plans.'

Abbott admitted to his ambassador that he had until then regretfully begun to accept Dyott's version of events, because the occasional stories that Fawcett was alive were too vague for credibility; but he felt Rattin's account was different. Abbott had borrowed the best maps available from the local agricultural and geographical commission and had tried to work out the exact position of the encounter, which Rattin described as being at a spot where the Iguassu Ximary (a tributary of the Rio São Manoel) meets a smaller unnamed river at a point several miles south-west of the Rio São Manoel. Rattin gave the name of the Indian encampment as Bocaina, and thought the tribe were called Morcegos; but the latter word means 'bats' and Abbott commented 'I hear there is no such tribe although it is a general name for certain Indians who do their hunting at night'.

Abbott showed Rattin a photograph of Fawcett and he claimed to see a likeness. Abbott also had a recollection that Fawcett wore various rings, and Rattin declared that he had been wearing four and described them as having various coloured stones in them and one of them being a 'snake-ring'. (Brian Fawcett later commented that 'my father never wore such a collection of rings'.) Rattin also told Abbott that his

English colonel had shown him a locket with a photograph of a lady and two girls and Abbott reported that—although Fawcett only had one daughter—it was quite possible that 'a baby-boy with long hair was taken for a girl.' (Again, Brian Fawcett was less convinced and commented 'I don't think my father ever had a locket like the one Rattin describes.')

The former ambassador, by this stage comfortably settled into retirement at Kingston Hill in Surrey, was intrigued but dubious about Rattin. He wrote back to Abbott in March 1932, wondering why—if Rattin's colonel really was Fawcett—the latter had not written a few lines or given some token to prove his existence. Paget thought it odd that Fawcett should be held prisoner and Rattin allowed to leave. He also saw difficulties about financing and organizing a rescue party and thought it would be premature to raise Mrs Fawcett's hopes that her husband might be alive.

Another person to be informed about Rattin's story was Commander Dyott, whose own theories were directly challenged. Predictably, Dyott was very dismissive about Rattin: he suggested to Abbott that 'the man Rattin' was a dubious character whom he had 'known under various names', that 'he is inventing a good deal', that 'there is something about his eyes that is not quite right', that in a previous exploit 'he got $5000 under false pretenses', and that he had on occasion passed himself off as an Italian Count. In fact, Dyott—without ever having met him and from a distance of five thousand miles —declared Rattin a fraud. Abbott was furious, and wrote to his colleague in New York pointing out that Rondon had described Dyott's own expedition as a 'complete fiasco', that 'many lost explorers in the past have been discovered on much flimsier evidence than I have about Fawcett', and that 'it is strange how some people have nothing better to do but to try to queer one's pitch.' The debate was becoming shrill.

Clearly the only person who could prove that Rattin had discovered Fawcett was Rattin. Only he could refind the undefined point south-west of the Rio São Manoel where the Morcegos were thought to be holding their English colonel. The Consul-General in São Paulo passed him on to his colleague in Rio who arranged a confrontation between Rattin and the celebrated General Rondon. The interview, which took three hours, was not a success. The Consul-General reported to Sir William Seeds:

'The General's . . . overpowering manner did not make it easy for Rattin, who held his own very well, however. Rondon said to Rattin that although he was very sceptical he was quite prepared to accompany him to the place where he says he saw the English Colonel. Rattin . . . said he much preferred to go alone with his friends. The General thereupon offered to supply him with mules, firearms, ammunition, provisions, equipment etc., but Rattin tells me that he does not want any money in advance. He says he is determined to free Fawcett and wants to return to Mato Grosso as soon as possible in order to do things in his own way. He hopes to succeed and get the reward for the "English Colonel" afterwards. He only came to us because he promised he would.'

Consul-General Goodwin in Rio was as convinced as Consul-General Abbott in São Paulo that Rattin was genuine and very possibly had indeed found Fawcett. Indeed he reported that it would be very difficult to keep Rattin more than a day or two in Rio because he said he must start his rescue operation at once in order to avoid the rainy season in Mato Grosso. Furthermore, an official of the Royal Bank of Canada who knew Fawcett well told Goodwin that he was greatly impressed by Rattin's description of the man and said he remembered distinctly that Fawcett had a gold ring in the shape of a snake with ruby eyes.

Goodwin was correct in at least one respect: there was to be no holding Rattin. He collected two companions, returned to the tiny town of Porto Velho in the heart of the Amazon forests (it is now capital of the new state of Rondônia named after the explorer and General) and set off in the direction of the encampment where he claimed to have encountered his Colonel. Neither Rattin nor either of his companions were ever seen or heard of again. He had backed his judgement with his life—and lost.

The Rattin affair was far from being the only rumoured news of the fate of Colonel Fawcett. An American missionary called Miss Martha Moennich wrote to Fawcett's widow claiming she had discovered an illegitimate son of Jack Fawcett in the depths of Xingu forests; a white child was brought out of the jungle to be reunited with 'his family', who—not surprisingly—were unimpressed and considered that the child was probably an albino in any case. Miss Moennich had collected her own version of how Rimmell had died of insect bites and how Colonel and Jack Fawcett had eventually been killed by Kalapolos Indians, when they insisted on pressing on, to save them from the worse fate of starving to death in the jungle. An Italian called Realini claimed to have found three skeletons belonging to the Fawcett party, but his tale failed to convince Mrs Fawcett or anyone else. Hardly a year went by in the 1930s without some new *canard*, but since the collapse of the 'bones' theory in the 1950s there has been a final resignation to a mystery which will remain a mystery.

And yet, who can resist his own speculation? For my own part (having read reports which—though available—appear not to have been studied or quoted before) I feel that Rattin has been too readily dismissed. It was not impossible that the ailing Rimmell *might* have been carried in nine days on one of the remaining animals over the 150 miles from Bakairi to a Dead Horse Camp at the map reference which Fawcett gave in his last letter to his wife. From my own observations of the terrain, it does not appear as impenetrable as has sometimes been suggested. The reasons for falsifying that final map reference seem unconvincing, and in his letter from Bakairi he refers to 'continuing north' which would more accurately describe his route to his own co-ordinates for Dead Horse Camp than to Dyott's supposed location for his camp. If Fawcett *was* so far north-west by that date, the possibility of his straying on to the São Manoel river (where Rattin found his Colonel) rather than on to the Kuluene river (where the false bones were found) seems much enhanced. Can much credence really be given to the collective 'confession' of the Kalapolos Indians twenty five years later to a 'crime' about which they had been subjected to so much cross-examination and invitation to elaborate? If Rattin was inventing his tale, how could he have known about Paget and the rings? (It seems likely that the two independent witnesses who recall Fawcett wearing them saw him *after* his son Brian had last seen him without them.) And would Rattin have been likely to have convinced two such professionally sceptical commentators as the Consuls-General in São Paulo and Rio (Consuls are seldom gullible by the time they reach such posts) if he had been a fraud and a liar? And—most emphatically of all—*why* should Rattin have invented such a tale: he asked for no fame or fortune, and went back to pursue his quest at the cost of his own life.

Perhaps, just possibly, the ageing mystic, soldier and explorer eked out his last lonely days among his nocturnally-active captors, pining for the son who 'was sleeping' and waiting for the little Swiss trapper to return and prove himself —after all—'a gentleman'.

8

THE LITERARY MEN

In August 1933 a bombshell hit the London literary scene. A young man, recently down from Oxford and currently acting as literary editor of the *Spectator* and occasional correspondent of *The Times*, published a travel book about a journey through Mato Grosso to look for Colonel Fawcett. The articles upon which people had expected the book to be based had appeared in *The Times* some months previously; they had excited some interest but no particular surprise; the expedition had been described in the way such expeditions were customarily described—informatively and without humour.

But when *Brazilian Adventure* by Peter Fleming emerged from Jonathan Cape's publishing house it caused a sensation. Almost without exception leading critics of the day commented on its new approach to adventurous travel which had, until then, been treated in a solemn, awe-inspiring, instructive or heroic manner. The great travellers of the nineteenth century —men like Burton, Stanley, Doughty and the myriad host of their lesser disciples—had been admired for their courage, their tenacity and their perspicacity, but hardly for their humour. They had made the most of their experiences in their books: streams had been rushing torrents, cliffs had been precipices, natives tended to be dangerous savages, swamps and chasms had been bottomless, thirst had been parching and dust blinding. Instruction had been conveyed explicitly and didactically. The tradition had been carried forward unchallenged into the twentieth century: Roosevelt and Rondon wrote of Amazonas much as Bates and Wallace had done.

Now a whole new phenomenon was suddenly exposed to the London literary critics. J. B. Priestley identified 'a unique blend of disillusion, foolhardiness and high spirits'; Harold Nicolson wrote of 'the slim neatness' of Fleming's style; David Garnett referred to a 'most delightful sense of humour', and the greatest pundit of them all—James Agate—pronounced it 'the adventure book one always dreams of reading and no-one ever writes'. Indeed, no-one ever had.

What had happened? The fact was that a year before Peter Fleming, then aged twenty-four, had responded on a whim to an advertisement in the personal column of *The Times*:

> 'Exploring and sporting expedition, under experienced guidance, leaving England June, to explore rivers central Brazil, if possible ascertain fate Colonel Fawcett; abundance game, big and small; exceptional fishing; ROOM TWO MORE GUNS; highest references expected and given. —Write Box X, *The Times*, E.C.4.'

He had managed to persuade a fellow Etonian friend to join the expedition with him and to get himself appointed as *The Times* correspondent to a venture for which, in his own words, 'Rider Haggard might have written the plot and Conrad designed the scenery'.

From the first it became clear that this was not to be like other Amazon expeditions. Amateurism was its keynote. Roosevelt and others might have been new to Amazonian travel, but they had usually had relevant experiences elsewhere and they had had professionals like Rondon with them; Fleming and his companions were not only new to any exploration of any sort, but instead of having a Rondon figure with them they were 'under the experienced guidance' of Captain J. G. Holman—a gentleman whom Fleming was to characterize as a total fraud once they had left civilization behind them.

To make matters worse, there were fundamental differences in objective between the various members of the expedition.

Fleming and his fellow Etonian friend were serious in their desire to make a genuine attempt to get into the region in which Fawcett had disappeared, and to make some attempt to throw light on his fate; it was—after all—only seven years since he had disappeared and not impossible that some information (even if not the man himself) might turn up. Captain Holman and most of the other members of the expedition had no intention of hazarding themselves to the same degree; for them, the shooting and fishing in exotic surroundings were the main attraction.

They all went overland from Rio de Janeiro to São Paulo (where their progress was temporarily halted by the outbreak of a revolution) and then up-country by lorry to the small town of Leopoldina on the Araguaya river. The Araguaya runs more or less due north for nearly 1500 miles, forming the border between the states of Mato Grosso and Goyas, merging first into the Tocantins and ultimately into the Amazon. It was down this river that the expedition planned to go as far as the mouth of the Tapirapé which flows into the Araguaya from the west (Mato Grosso) bank; they then planned to go up the Tapirapé and then strike over land towards the Kuluene river. Somewhere in the 200-odd miles between these two last-named rivers, they reckoned they would be passing close to the area where Fawcett had disappeared (see map).

All went reasonably well on the Araguaya: for three weeks they canoed down-stream, shooting birds and alligators, fishing, and camping on sandbanks. But when they reached the Tapirapé, Captain Holman had clearly had enough: he turned back to the Araguaya and left the young Englishmen to go on without their leader. This they did till they reached a small landing place four days by boat up the river. There they split: Fleming and his Etonian friend—joined by yet a third Etonian —decided to press on on foot to make contact with the Tapirapé tribesmen in the hope of finding guides who could lead them into the heart of the Fawcett country; the rest of the

party decided to go on by canoe further up the Tapirapé river
and map its hitherto uncharted course.

The river party spent a few relatively uneventful days and
returned down the Tapirapé to rejoin Captain Holman on the
Araguaya. But Fleming and his companions had a more
exciting time. They even managed to secure the services of
some self-styled 'chiefs', whose local knowledge was non-existent once they left the immediate area of their tribe, and whose
apprehension of their neighbouring tribes was infectious.

Eventually, after some further days of wading up streams,
cutting their way through thickets, eating up almost the last of
their rations, being deserted by their guides and seeing the
smoke from the fires of unknown Indians retreating ever
further in front of them, they decided that honour was satisfied
and turned back—none the wiser about Fawcett.

The small party who had accompanied Fleming on this
—the most adventurous—leg of the journey now paddled
down the Tapirapé again to its confluence with the Araguaya;
they had four very hungry days before they rejoined Captain
Holman and the rest of the expedition, who were encamped on
a sand-bank near the mouth of the Tapirapé. Then the real
drama started. Holman was furious at what he saw as Fleming's insubordination and defection in taking off with a part of
the expedition to attempt to achieve its objective when he,
Holman, had declared this to be impracticable. He firstly
refused even to speak to Fleming and his friends, and then
informed them that—by taking off on their own and resigning
from his expedition—they had forfeited both any claim on his
further help and their passage money home; he intended to
abandon them—with one canoe and very little food and no
money—to find their own way a thousand miles down-river to
the Amazon. If they needed funds, Holman declared, they
could sell the canoe; but he did not suggest how they might
continue the journey in that eventuality. Fleming characteristically recalls—with more humour than rancour—his shock at

Holman's drastic reaction to their escapade; he had expected that

> 'Our relations would be strained; but I did not anticipate that (Holman) would sever them altogether. I had always under-stood, from the *Wide World Magazine* and other authorities, that in the Great Open Spaces this sort of thing was never done, however much you wanted it; there was a thing called The Unwritten Law which prevented you from doing it. So I did not seriously contemplate the possibility of (Holman) withdrawing from us not only his society but his assistance, and not only his assistance but our own funds, on the long and rather difficult journey down to Pará. But (Captain Holman), it turned out, had never even heard of the Unwritten Law.'

Eventually, after mobilizing other members of the expedition and intermediaries and threatening Holman with dire ex-posure, Fleming managed to persuade him to do 'what in this sort of story is called the Big Thing' and pass over the princely sum of ten pounds.

From then on it was a race between Fleming and his friends, and Captain Holman and his supporters; both parties were desperately anxious to descend the Araguaya to civilization before the other, and so to be able to get in first with their own account of why the expedition had split up and what had happened. It was a close-run and—in Fleming's account —hilarious race, with first one and then the other party taking the lead over the thousand-mile course. Fleming's party won.

The arrival of the two acrimonious factions in Belém caused a good deal of bother to the British consul, who commented tersely in October that 'the expedition proved a complete fiasco, with the result that the members quarrelled and broke up ... on the arrival of the two antagonized sections in Pará (Belém) I contrived to arrange a provisional agreement which enabled the members of the expedition to reach their respective destinations without recourse to public funds, in spite of the impecunious condition in which they almost all reached this city'. Consular honour had been satisfied.

But the quarrel rumbled on. Holman, with the help of the three other members of the party who were 'loyal' to him, prepared his own version of the breach and the reasons for it. It is an angrily argued document* and attacks Fleming in particular. Holman starts by rebutting the charge that he had broken faith by failing to make 'a thorough and genuine search for traces of Colonel Fawcett'. He claims that:

'No matter what he (Holman) may have outlined as his plans in Rio, São Paulo, and even as late as when in Goyaz, events in Brazil, incidents occurring whilst going down river, and the behaviour and physical fitness of certain members of the party, entirely justified him in his refusal to sanction an inland march from the river Tapirapé.'

Holman goes on to claim that Fleming approached him with the proposition that he and two of the others (his Etonian friends) should 'make the full attempt', while the others should remain behind either on the Araguaya or on the Tapirapé, and that Holman consented to this scheme. Holman's paper goes on:

'Even before Holman had an opportunity of denying the truth of this accusation, Fleming had thus, on his own showing, secretly consented to become a party to one of the most discreditable acts in the annals of such expeditions. He, and his friend Pettiward, had enrolled themselves as members in a band of men, bound together on a common mission. Yet at one of the first opportunities they indulged in an intrigue, whereby they were to gain any honour and kudos

---

* The author has been shown copies which were circulated at the time in São Paulo, but it is believed that this is the first time it has been quoted in print.

that there was to be acquired, at the expense of their comrades. When taxed with this, Fleming claimed that the idea had originated with Holman . . . Holman himself, indignantly denies ever to have entered into such a pact with Fleming.'

Holman's paper then goes on to argue that it was 'particularly despicable' of Fleming to have proposed such a plan because he was—on account of his contract with *The Times*—the only member of the expedition whose financial recompense was assured and that this had been made possible by his nomination as special correspondent by one of those whom he intended to leave behind: 'no extenuating circumstances can be advanced for such ingratitude', he thunders.

The paper then addressed itself to whether Holman ever intended 'to provide for any cross-country march in search of the information about Fawcett', and concludes that he did, but that he changed his mind. It claims that Holman 'was so entitled by the written undertaking of every member to obey his orders and to respect his decisions.' This is a slight *non sequitur*: while the written undertaking may have obliged the members of the expedition to follow any changed plan which Holman adumbrated, it hardly justified Holman himself in deviating from the declared intention of the whole enterprise. But the paper goes on to explain why Holman did so deviate. Firstly, he blames the revolution which broke out while they were in São Paulo 'which entailed considerable extra time and expense in getting the personnel and baggage of the expedition up to Goyaz'. Then it claims that the majority of the valuable stores and foodstuffs sent on ahead had gone astray as a result of the revolution, and that although some of these losses were made good, others could not be—not least for lack of funds. The paper becomes very defensive on the question of those food supplies and maintains that it was not true that Holman deliberately under-supplied the expedition to provide a reason for not pressing on overland. Another *non sequitur* gives as evidence of this the fact that food never ran short on the restricted itinerary which they fulfilled. Finally, the paper adduces the argument that 'even had the expedition possessed a greater quantity of supplies, it would have been impossible to have stayed longer on the Tapirapé, because the rivers were steadily drying up', and follows this in the same sentence with the conflicting (and rather more valid) argument that 'the rainy season was approaching'. Such a welter of inconsequent and inconsistent reasoning falls some way short of carrying total conviction.

The paper next attacks Fleming for taking one of the Brazilian hired hands with them, without Holman's consent. 'It seems this man never really knew what he was letting himself in for, either; due to Fleming's limited command of the language.' Explaining why Holman refused to accept Fleming's formal resignation from the expedition, the paper recounts how Fleming and his friends had gone off on their own anyway and 'left Holman in the lurch, and in addition taken one of his best workers with them.' Then follows the final rationalization of what, in Fleming's narrative, was to seem the ultimate enormity of Holman's behaviour:

'After several days—anxious ones for Holman—they returned and expected to be treated as if nothing had happened. Holman gave them a boat, half the stores, a sufficient sum of money, and told them to get to Belém by themselves, as he wished to have nothing further to do with them, and they would forfeit their passages home since they had resigned from the expedition.'

This was not at all how Fleming had seen the incident which he had so vividly described in *Brazilian Adventure*.

But beyond grousing to the consul in Belém, and to anyone else who would listen, and ensuring that he got enough money for his return fare to England, Fleming did not exploit his arrival ahead of Holman to present his version of events to the

British public. Indeed, when his unremarkable articles, already referred to, appeared in *The Times* it seemed that, neither in its achievements nor in its resultant journalism, had the expedition been anything very out of the usual.

Why then did the book that followed create such a splash? The short answer is that it was both iconoclastic and very funny. All the long-held attitudes towards exploration, and more particularly towards the Amazon, were exploded in a series of brilliant fireworks.

To start with, he was not overawed by the wild life, particularly not by alligators which he declares to be 'a fraud . . . all my eye and Sir John Mandeville'. Fleming lightheartedly describes the terrible aspect of the alligator but ends by admitting:

'For two months we saw him every day; we slept within reach of him, we swam in his waters. He was content to look malign and live on his reputation . . . perhaps we expected too much from alligators'.

And it was not only alligators that drew his disdain: 'As a matter of fact, most of the terrors of the Central Brazilian jungle had a way of paling into rather ludicrous insignificance when you looked at them closely.'

And look at them closely he did. The dreaded reputation of the piranha fish did not prevent Fleming and his companions from wading all day among them on the tributaries of the Tapirapé.

'We could not but admire the rigid self-control which ruled their blood-lust . . . sometimes a small shoal would approach . . . staring at our legs with a wistful, perhaps a slightly covetous awe: as shop girls gaze at the sentries outside Buckingham Palace.'

He concludes that walking among them in the Tapirapé was scarcely more dangerous than walking through a farm yard of poultry, and confesses himself at a loss to know why this should be so unless it was that 'human beings were so rare an item of their diet that among the shoals a lack of unanimity prevailed on the question of our value as food'. The sceptical passage did however end with a word of caution about going into the water in the proximity of piranha with a sore or a cut on one's leg.

Even the most fear-inspiring of all Amazon phenomena —the anaconda, which had so nearly brought Bates and others to a grisly end—does not arouse the customary awe in Fleming; he reports finding one sleeping in a hollow tree and being too tired to do anything about it apart from 'emptying a revolver lackadaisically' into the tree, which—he says—quickened the tempo of its hiss but produced no other result. He then went to sleep in the immediate proximity of this presumably wounded and enraged reptile.

Almost as proverbial in the annals of earlier writers as the hazards of the wild life, were the health hazards of central Brazil. But Fleming describes the Mato Grosso as more of a health resort than a White Man's Grave, and goes on to argue that its evil reputation is largely an excuse produced by Brazilians who do not want to go anywhere so uncomfortable.

As if undermining the traditional deterrents of jungle travel was not enough, Fleming also sets about undermining the mental attitudes and vocabulary of earlier explorers. He condemns as an affectation what he calls 'the *Nullah* (or Ravine) School of Literature', by which he means the tendency of travellers to use native words in italics to describe phenomena for which a perfectly adequate English word exists. Why—he argues—should a hillock be a *kopje*, or a stockade a *zareba*?

Indeed he goes further than this, and explains at some length how he and his Etonian friends deliberately and ironically adopted for use between themselves the full panoply of nineteenth-century explorers' purple prose. They never said 'Was that a shot?' but always 'Was that the well-known bark of a Mauser?' They spoke of water always as the 'Precious Fluid'.

They referred to themselves, not as eating meals, but as doing 'Ample justice to a Frugal Repast'. When Indians approached them they referred to them as 'Oncoming Savages'. As Fleming himself admits, it must have been a maddening way to carry on for those of the party who did not relish the joke. But when he recounts this verbal irreverence to the *mores* of generations of earlier travellers in wildernesses of the world, he is putting yet another nail in the coffin of the previously accepted attitude towards the Amazon and all who adventured on its waters.

In most respects Fleming's book is one of the most truthful accounts ever written of Amazonian travel: not only is exaggeration eschewed, but it is replaced by modest understatement. Yet in one important respect Fleming had to depart from truth in the interests of avoiding law suits: this was in his treatment of Captain Holman. The problem was that the captain's cowardice, duplicity and bad temper were an integral part of the story. Indeed, had it not been for these alleged characteristics in their leader, the party would certainly never have split and might well have reached the area where genuine intelligence about Fawcett's fate might have been gleaned. But if Fleming had attributed to Holman the unattractive and disruptive qualities which he had so amply described, Holman might well have sued him and his publishers for libel, as Holman was a well-known figure in São Paulo who looked forward to future earnings from taking other parties of adventurers on sporting safaris to Mato Grosso. And so, (as Duff Hart-Davis has revealed in his authoritative and fascinating life of Peter Fleming*) Fleming decided to divide Captain Holman into two Jekyll and Hyde characters: the responsible leader of the expedition who negotiates the travel arrangements up-country is allowed to keep his own name of Captain J. G. Holman; but the tiresome liar and fraud who frustrates their further progress up the Tapirapé is dubbed 'Major

* *Peter Fleming: A biography* (London 1974).

Pingle'. The device worked admirably: the story was not watered down, and the prospect of facing legal action was averted.

Fleming's modesty extended even to the choice of title. He considered 'Trespassers in Hell' and 'Brazil through the Agony Column' but rejected both as too dramatic, perhaps feeling that the former title was also too reminiscent of Hardenburg's account of his exposures on the Putamayo—'The Devil's Paradise'. Something had been started which was not to end with him.

In December of the same year—1932—that saw Peter Fleming making his trip down the Araguaya, another young English writer—his reputation resting mainly on a single satirical novel—set out to approach the Amazon from the opposite direction from Fleming.

Evelyn Waugh sailed for Georgetown on the coast of what was then British Guiana with no very clear idea of the journey he wished to make, beyond a general intention to penetrate into the interior of the country, cross the frontier into Brazil and make his way down the Rio Blanco to Manaus and thence down the Amazon and home. The trip was even more of a failure than Fleming's attempt to find Fawcett: Waugh did not even get riverbound on the Rio Blanco, let alone reach Manaus.

Waugh had not yet read *Brazilian Adventure*, but a lot of his attitudes towards travel in Amazonas were, if not the same as Fleming's, at least similar in many significant respects. Like Fleming—for instance—he explicitly disclaims that his mission had any high motive of exploration or scientific discovery. He opens his first chapter with 'an apology for the book I am going to write' and goes on to explain that 'there are no hairbreadth escapes, no romances, no discoveries . . . it seems presumptuous to suppose I shall interest anyone.' The worlds of Bates' instructive observations, and of Roosevelt's heroic narrations are—once again—left far behind us.

Waugh does not share that ebullient enthusiasm which makes Fleming's trip from first to last a light-hearted escapade. Indeed, where Fleming exults in the absurdity of the situations that confront him—delays, obfuscating officials, the prevalence of misinformation—Waugh tends to become irritated and crotchety. But with both writers the greatest interest of the book is not what happens to them, but how they react to what happens. It is the process of literary digestion of material, rather than the material itself, which holds the reader's attention and explains the repeated reprinting of the books. Waugh is more aware of this process than Fleming. He puts his finger on it early on in the book when he writes 'For myself . . . there is a fascination in distant and barbarous places . . . it is there that I find the experiences vivid enough to demand translation into literary form.' His self-examination is at the same time both more self-conscious and more profound than Fleming's.

But both of them have the same faintly disdainful attitude to that formidable wild life which so impressed their forerunners. While Fleming is forever belittling the dangers of alligators, piranha fish and snakes, Waugh is more detached and dismissive. He casually observes that jaguars and buck slink away from his path, and when his approach obliges a python to disgorge a large toad which it is in the process of swallowing, his attention is more on the victim than the predator: the python 'slipped away' while 'the toad showed little gratitude or surprise at his escape, but dragged himself rather laboriously under a log and sat down to consider his experience'. Wallace or Bates would not have let the many-coiled monster slip off their pages so easily.

The real dangers and horrors which preoccupied earlier travellers – cannibals, carnivorous animals, poisonous reptiles —were replaced in Waugh's case by the horror of boredom. The most poignant passage in *Ninety Two Days* describes the disappointment of reaching Boa Vista, the small town to the north of the Amazon, after the high expectations of it which had been built up in his mind:

> 'Whatever I had looked for in vain at Figuiredo's store was, he told me, procurable at "Boa Vist"'; Mr Daguar had extolled its modernity and luxury—electric light, cafés, fine buildings, women, politics, murders. Mr Bain had told of the fast motor launches, plying constantly between there and Manaus. In the discomfort of the journey there, I had looked forward to the soft living of Boa Vista . . .'

But when he got there the reality could not have been more different. The natives had an air which suggested that 'only listlessness kept them from active insult'. There was nowhere to stay as 'strangers do not come to Boa Vist''. When he asks whether the appearance of the promised launches to Manaus will be a question of days or weeks, he is told 'a question of weeks or months'. He outstays his welcome with the tolerant Benedictine monks. He loses patience with all and sundry. He runs out of reading material. This is the frustration of a sophisticated literary man faced with inconvenience of discomfort, discourtesy and delay: it bears little relation to the ordeals of adventurers, explorers and naturalists of former epochs.

Not only does Waugh disparage the attitude of earlier travellers in Amazonas, he disparages the attitudes of traditional travellers to the whole business of travelling. He lists a number of conventional fallacies, such as that the traveller is untrammelled by convention, and comments 'surely it is easier to remember the few rules of conduct in which one has been trained from the nursery, than to adapt oneself to the unpredictable politenesses, the often nauseating hospitality of savages?' He contests the accepted wisdom that the traveller in the wild has a healthy appetite and sleeps like a child, maintaining that he could not stomach the food available on his own trip and that he scarcely had a single good night's sleep in the open. As for 'feeling free', he declares that every personal possession became an incumbrance. Waugh was in fact an intrepid traveller, but presented himself as an anti-traveller, in the same sense that the heroes of his novels were to be so often anti-heroes.

Waugh ends as he begins—with disclaimers. 'The journey was over and the book might as well come to an end. There is no occasion for a purple passage.' But the Amazon had exerted its forceful influence on him no less surely than on those who had written of it, in earlier centuries, with more awe and reverence. When he came to write *A Handful of Dust*, he sent his hero—Tony Last—into the depths of Amazons to end his days in macabre confinement, reading Dickens aloud to a mad eccentric who refuses to release him. (Waugh himself had been reading *Nicholas Nickleby* during his own journey.) It is as if, even in fiction, he finds it necessary to mock the mighty forests that had daunted so many of his predecessors.

It was ironic that within months of his return, and before he sat down to write his own book, Waugh found himself reviewing *Brazilian Adventure* for the *Spectator*. He must inevitably have realized that this seminal book ended a centuries old convention of how to approach travel in Amazonas (and indeed elsewhere). He praised the book highly, but criticized Fleming for 'going to the extreme limits of depreciation in his anxiety to avoid the pretentious . . . he is afraid to let himself go . . . he is afraid of purple passages.' Maybe. But Waugh himself, when he settled down to write up his own trip just two months later, was to demonstrate many of these self-same characteristics of depreciation.

The heroics of Amazon travel had been lost—like Colonel Fawcett—in the aftermath of the First World War. They were not to be refound until the 1950s.

9

THE DEVELOPERS

Until the 1920s, British and North American interest in the Amazon had been almost exclusively restricted to that of would-be settlers, of explorers or of naturalists. Rubber was viewed as a wild crop, and its exploitation left to the natives of Brazil or neighbouring Amazonian countries. Not since the earliest days of the seventeenth century had there been any Anglo-Saxon attempt to take over tracts of the Amazon forest —and, even then, the emphasis had been on settlement rather than development. All that was now to change.

In 1926, Henry Ford—the motor tycoon of Detroit— unexpectedly turned his intensive but quirky gaze on the Amazon. He reasoned that the Amazon forests were the traditional home of the rubber tree; that if the carefully nurtured plantations of south-east Asia could produce so much latex, then how much better such methods would flourish in the original habitat of the rubber plant; that he was the largest motor-car producer in the world and therefore the biggest customer for rubber tyres; that he had the capital and imagination to launch a project that would at one and the same time transform the Amazon basin and give him a permanent domination over the world's rubber supply. It was—to say the least—an eccentric idea.

But by 1926, Mr Ford had established a reputation for eccentricity which went far beyond the confines of Detroit, the state of Michigan, or even the United States of America. He had become a legend in his own time, and not an altogether attractive one—a man of paradoxes and inconsistencies. He had made a practice of paying his work force well above the standard rates, but he resisted unionization of his work by every means fair and foul—including employing spies and thugs on the factory floor. He had made an additional fortune out of transport contracts in the First World War, had voluntarily offered—a singular act of generosity—to give the profits back to the US government, and had then forgotten or overlooked the offer. He had shown extraordinary loyalty to some of his senior managers, and had inexplicably turned against others—not only sacking them overnight but taking the roofs off their offices, chopping up their office furniture and virtually maintaining that they had never existed. He had diagnosed the popular need for mobility and had produced cheap cars to meet it, but he had drawn the line at allowing his customers to choose the colour of car they wanted: 'they can have any colour they want as long as it's black'. He had swum with the tide of history while publicly declaring that 'history is bunk'.

This was the man who decided to swamp the world market with his Amazonian rubber. It was not to be a tentative venture, but from the start a massive takeover bid for control of the world's rubber market*. Ford bought one million hectares (nearly two and a half million acres) of the Amazon forest from the government of the state of Pará and soon afterwards purchased a further one and a half million hectares. At the same time he negotiated a 'tax-holiday' on his profits for the next fifty years. The vast tract of land which he purchased lay along the Tapajós river, one of the main southerly tributaries of the Amazon which it joins at Santarém. His personal identification with the scheme, and the almost-national scale of the enterprise were both reflected in the grandiose name he gave to the project: Fordlandia.

Ford set in hand the clearance of large areas of jungle and the planting of a range of different varieties of Brazilian rubber

---

* The Goodyear and Firestone companies were so alarmed at the prospect that they immediately set in train plans for their own vast plantations in Costa Rica and Liberia.

plants—all of them related to the *hevea brasiliensis* seeds which Wickham had stolen from exactly this area just fifty years before. When the trees had grown to latex-bearing stature, Ford reckoned that the target production of Fordlandia should be 40,000 tons of raw latex a year. The ambitious nature of this target figure is illustrated by the fact that its achievement would have more than doubled the whole world's production of rubber at that date. But Ford reckoned that this was not unrealistic in view of the fact that he was planning to plant an area larger than all the existing British and Dutch plantations in Malaya, Sumatra and the entire Far East put together.

But from the start there were problems, as there have usually been with projects which involve the rapid de-forestation of Amazonas. When the original tall jungle trees were felled, there was an immediate decrease in the amount of moisture and an immediate increase in the amount of sunlight. The soil proved to be less deep and rich than might have been supposed from the thick verdure with which it had been covered. The *hevea brasiliensis*, which had flourished so well while growing wild and interspersed among the other taller trees of the forest, faltered when left to grow in isolation. Seven years after its dramatic inauguration, Fordlandia was producing less than five per cent of its initial target figure.

Henry Ford still thought that his original concept was a sound one, but was prepared to concede that he was experiencing a little local difficulty. He concluded that the answer was to swap his land-holding at Fordlandia for an equally large area a few miles further north at Belterra, also on the Tapajós river and even nearer to Santarém. This time he would not restrict his planting to the Brazilian seedlings, but would use the Far Eastern plantation trees that had been refined from the original *hevea brasiliensis*.

Nothing daunted, he doubled his investment and began again. To show seriousness of purpose he also set up a complete social structure at Belterra: a hospital was built;

public utlities were installed; sports facilities—including a golf course—were laid out; schools were constructed; a church was dedicated; and a hotel was provided for the hoped-for visitors and admirers from all over the world. Recalling the troubles he had had in the past at Detroit, he even instituted his own police force and he paid his workers well over the local rates. Although not carrying the Ford family name as the earlier estate had done, Belterra none-the-less incorporated the Ford principles and practices.

But the change of location did not solve the problems. The imported seedlings did not like the heat any more than the local ones; nor was the soil at Belterra substantially richer or more stable than further south. If anything, the young trees seemed to be even more vulnerable to infectious diseases here than at Fordlandia: leaf mould alone killed off fifteen per cent of the trees, and not more than half of the three million which were planted produced any latex at all—the rest being stunted failures. Even the productive trees never performed as well as the same species did in Malaya and Sumatra. Possibly the trees lacked attention in the formative period because, despite all his inducements, Ford had great difficulty in persuading the easy-going inhabitants of Santarém to work on his model estate. Whatever the reasons, by 1941, despite monumental efforts by Henry Ford himself and his management team and even with the added incentive of rising world demand for rubber in the Second World War, the total production had only risen to some ten per cent of his original target.

Ford realized at last that he would never dominate the world's rubber supply from his base in the Amazon forests; he would never even produce all the rubber he needed for Ford tyres; he would never be hailed as the great developer of the world's greatest river bank. Even the buffaloes on the ranch he had set up were being killed by jaguars. He was losing money and losing face. As soon as the Second World War was over, in December 1945, he sold up. It has been estimated that in all he invested some eighty million US dollars in Fordlandia and Belterra; he accepted a quarter of a million dollars from the state government of Pará—some 0.3 per cent of his money back. The dramatic proportions of the failure might have been expected to act as a warning to other American tycoons that liberties were not to be lightly taken with the virgin forests of the Amazon; but any such warning had not reached the 70-year-old president of National Bulk Carriers, in his Manhattan headquarters, by 1967.

Daniel K. Ludwig was American by birth and by character. His family came from Germany but he himself was born at South Haven in Michigan in 1897. By 1967 he was convincingly described as a billionaire and one of the world's richest men, and his fortune—like Henry Ford's—was the result of his own imagination, energy and financial daring. He claims to have started his shipping interests when he was nine years old by salvaging a sunken boat, and indeed shipping was to be the basis—but not the perimeter—of his industrial empire. During the Second World War, flying in the face of all maritime and financial advice, he started constructing oil-tankers twice the size of those of his competitors. From 30,000-tonners, he progressed to supertankers. He established his own shipyard at Kure, in southern Japan, and—in the words of the Japanese Emperor—'revitalized the whole Japanese shipbuilding industry'. He undertook other engineering feats related to shipping such as dredging the Orinoco River in Venezuela (which may first have turned his mind to the Amazon); and he also undertook projects in quite different fields—mining, construction, ranching. He had operations in fifteen different countries and a house in Beverly Hills, California.

One common thread ran through Ludwig enterprises: they were forward-looking. Born in the nineteenth century, he none-the-less prided himself on turning his mind towards what would be the requirements of the world in the twenty-first century. By the 1960s he was convinced that the world communications explosion would cause a shortage of paper (however much radio and television might help to absorb the explosion) and that the bottle-neck would be wood-pulp. To produce wood-pulp fast it was necessary to grow trees fast. For Ludwig this meant not just identifying a fast-growing tree, but identifying the *fastest*. So he sent out expert scouts round the world to report back to him on the possibilities. Eventually one of them returned in 1965 with a report on *gmelina arborea* more commonly known and pronounced as the melina tree; this was proved to be growing at the phenomenal rate of over a foot a month in Nigeria, where it had been introduced from Burma to provide pit-props for the west-African gold mines. Melina apparently did well in Panama too. Ludwig was convinced it was the answer: an all-purpose, 'instant', tropical timber.

The next problem was to identify a location for his plantations. Again, the scouts went out. Again, they were told to search quickly. By 1967 they reported back that there was a Portuguese trading company with a large land holding on the banks of the Jari river, a northern tributary near the mouth of the Amazon; the owners appeared to do little with the land except collect nuts from the forests and do some ranching with cattle and buffalo along the river's edge. Ludwig's scouts explored the terrain in canoes and on mule-back. They confirmed that there was access for deep-draught ships up the Jari river and that it was unlikely that labour costs would be high in a part of Brazil with rapidly-expanding population centres nearby and relatively low living standards. When Ludwig came down to Brazil himself, he liked what he found: a stable government, a friendly President, a welcome for massive foreign investment, and no demands for state participation. Ludwig promptly bought four million acres of Jari for three million dollars; he can little have guessed that he was going to keep pumping money in at an average rate of nearly $200,000 *a day* for the next fourteen years.

Speed had been the hallmark of the whole operation, and it was to remain so. The first objective was to cut down the forest to make room to plant the melina. In the initial stages, little thought was given to salvaging those trees which might have a value of their own, or even to determining what was being cut down; conservationists protested that unknown species of flora were possibly being burnt up in a general scorched-earth policy. Ludwig himself was sceptical: he doubted the fragility of the Amazon's ecosystem and was quoted* as saying 'Hell's bells, I spend five million dollars a year just to whack down the wild growth that springs up among our planted trees.' When Ludwig's forest fires started causing thunder-storms some miles away, then other environmentalists protested that the climate of the Amazon—and ultimately, they argued, of the world—would be affected. Be that as it might, the melina seedlings were stretching to the horizon as early as 1969 and soon shipments of tree-trunks were going off to pulp-mills in Scandinavia—some of them still sprouting greenery as they went to such an alarming degree that the Finnish dockers insisted that the cargoes were searched for snakes before they would handle them.

But, as with Henry Ford's rubber striplings, all was not well. The soil left behind after the forest was cleared was too thin. Heavy bull-dozing machinery could not be used without further disrupting the sub-soil, so more labour-intensive methods of clearance were necessary. Local contractors brought in more labour from the impoverished areas of north-eastern Brazil and there were reports that they were being fed on monkey-meat. Even when the heavy clearing machinery had been replaced with human labour, the remaining soil though no longer impacted was frequently too sandy for

* by the *National Geographic Magazine* of May 1980.

melina. The newly-made roads were washed away by the 100 inches of annual rainfall. Pests attacked the young plants: the leaf-mould which had attacked Ford's rubber found an equivalent in the leaf-cutter ants that attacked Ludwig's melina.

Just as Ford had switched from the indigenous rubber plants to other varieties, so Ludwig now diversified out of melina into other trees. He planted fast growing eucalyptus and—somewhat reluctantly—pine ('anyone can grow pine'). And like Ford he pumped in ever more money.

To stop the criticisms of the way his labour force was treated, he built a model town. His Belterra was called Monte Dourado. It too had all the modern, hygienic amenities; indeed, so antiseptic did it appear to many Brazilians that they preferred to set up camp on the opposite side of the Jari river and a bustling, water-side shanty-town quickly grew up at Beiradão. Here there were no roads and few utilities, but plenty of bars, gambling-dens and other frontier-town haunts for casual workers. Ludwig's timber yards and forests could be reached by canoeing across the river. Those who suspected that Ludwig might introduce his own Ford-like police force at Monte Dourado felt more comfortable amid the *caxaça*-soaked chaos of the early days at Beiradão.

By 1977, despite the funds he had already poured into Jari, Ludwig decided on his biggest gamble of all. He needed his own pulp-mill and a power-plant to operate it—a wood-burning power-plant that could run on the timber which Ludwig had earlier been burning up merely to clear the ground. Local construction would be immensely difficult and expensive, whereas he knew all about the attractions of production at Kure in Japan where he had built his own ships. The problem was transport. Ludwig—never one to be deterred by doing what had not been done before—decided that he would *float* the two huge factories involved from Kure to Jari—across the China seas and the Indian ocean, around the Cape of Good Hope, across the South Atlantic and finally up the Amazon (they were far too long and large to go the shorter route through the Panama Canal). The prospect would have daunted anyone else: the power-plant alone weighed over 30,000 tons, was the length of three football fields or average-sized city blocks, and stood over twenty storeys high. The pulp-mill was of similar proportions. The world's largest ocean-going tugs were harnessed to the task. The whole operation was achieved without serious hitch and when the two great factories were towed into a flooded area alongside the Jari river in April 1978, and the water ballast was removed, allowing them to settle on their rot-proof-timbered foundation, they were found to be perfectly aligned. Ludwig had achieved a notable victory over the hazards of the world's greatest oceans; he was to find the hazards of the world's greatest river-basin more difficult to overcome.

Plagues continued to beset him. Malaria, dysentery, yellow fever—those old enemies of the nineteenth-century explorers and naturalists—were still capable of flaring into occasional outbreaks, and one year a particularly virulent form of meningitis swept through Jari killing off some twenty employees before Ludwig managed to fly in a rare and effective vaccine. As fast as Ludwig diversified into other projects at Jari—a Kaolin clay mine, rice fields, more buffalo ranching—so fresh problems arose. His visits were frequent but often dreaded by his managerial staff; he would arrive at Jari exhausted but impatient after a fourteen-hour flight from New York (he always travelled by commercial airlines in economy class as a matter of principle); he would inspect pet projects; like Henry Ford, he would sack managers who had failed to meet his demanding deadlines; he would snap at those who queried the cost-effectiveness of what he was proposing: 'You worry about getting it done . . . I'll worry about the money.' And indeed, as each hundred million dollars succeeded the last and the total capital input neared one billion dollars, it seemed that the Ludwig coffers were bottomless.

But all the time, the Amazon's intractable qualities were eroding both Ludwig's energy and his fortune. He had always been secretive about his Jari empire: journalists were prohibited, interviews rarely given and access to the jungle fastness was only possible by flights or ships which he largely controlled (there was and is no road to Jari). As problems proliferated and more and more money was being injected from National Bulk Carriers and other interests, Ludwig began to suspect that there was a conspiracy against him. He knew that foreign development of the Amazon had been resented, as exploitation or plundering, since the seventeenth century; and now he introduced his own confidants as agents at Jari to watch how his instructions were being carried out and to report back directly to him—just as Henry Ford's 'spies' on the factory floor had done.

As finance got tighter, so wage rolls were cut down: there were no longer enough workers to weed between the trees and so timber production fell behind; melina crops from the sandy soil also gave disappointing results; there was soon not enough wood to keep the pulp-mill at full production. As conservation practices improved, and more of the useable timber was extracted from the felled forests, so the process of forest clearance slowed down and became more complex. As news of the problems leaked out—despite the press embargoes—so it became harder to raise fresh capital: the plan for damming the Jari river to produce hydro-electric power, and the plans for a paper-mill to supplement the pulp-mill, all had to be suspended.

Eventually and inevitably, Ludwig followed the course of Ford and sold out to the Brazilian government. Then—with fresh loans and new management—the project went forward, winning over the environmentalists and setting right the balance sheets; but it was no longer the private empire that its founder had envisaged. Another American fortune had come to grief on the banks of the Amazon: as *Fortune* magazine put it

'Ludwig's enthusiasm had cost him his billionaire status'. Another Anglo-Saxon had been made to feel an intruder in an alien world. Just as the Portuguese and Indians drove out the early English settlers, just as diseases eventually forced the withdrawal of the early English and American naturalists, just as the impenetrable forests and natural hazards crippled or swallowed up so many Anglo-Saxon explorers and adventurers ... so the peculiarly intractable Amazon had successfully resisted the inroads of the capitalists. Two giants of American industry, at home wherever they went in the world, had been made to feel trespassers on this river bank.

10

THE CONTEMPORARIES

However adventurous in a financial sense Mr Ford and Dr Ludwig might have been, theirs had not been a physical adventure. The mantle of Bates and Wallace, of Roosevelt and Fawcett, of Fleming and Waugh was to fall—in the second half of the twentieth century—on a new generation of young explorers who, in the best tradition of their predecessors, wrote lively accounts of their exploits. Like many activities, Amazonian travel has proliferated: this book has never claimed that its accounts of earlier Anglo-Saxon travellers was an exhaustive one, but with the passing of the decades in the present century it has been necessary to be ever more selective. Those whose adventures are recounted below are only a sample of the many who took to canoes and jungle tracks to penetrate what is still the world's largest region of obscurity: but I believe they are a sample of the boldest and the best.

In 1950, a young Englishman called Sebastian Snow, who had perhaps less reason than most of his contemporaries to hazard himself in remote forests, since he was still suffering from some ill-effects of a thigh which had been badly broken while at school at Eton, decided to travel from a point which he confidently claimed as the source of the Amazon in the Peruvian Andes, to its mouth at Belém some three and a half thousand miles away.

At first glance there was nothing particularly remarkable about travelling the length of the Amazon: as long ago as 1541, Francisco Orellana had left Pizarro's band of *conquistadors*—in what is now Ecuador—on what was intended to be a short foraging trip and—finding it difficult to return up-stream

—had persisted down-stream until he reached the Atlantic ocean. What made Snow's venture remarkable was that he started so high up the river and that he intended to keep to the actual valley of the Marañon (the Amazon's principal source, by his calculation) for 500 miles before the river was reckoned to become navigable. The first 1,300 miles of his journey took him over nine months to accomplish.

The first stage of the journey had to be made by pony and on foot, because—as Snow explains in his own account of his travels*—'we clung like limpets to the bends and turns of the rushing, raging Marañon,' which at this altitude was of the magnitude of a trout stream and too insubstantial, as well as too turbulent, for navigation even by raft or canoe.

But when the river widened, Snow decided that he ought to travel on the water and not beside it, despite the reported prevalence of rapids and whirlpools. The best conveyance appeared to be a balsa-wood raft. Even on this it would be only remotely possible to attempt the passage in April, and Snow had reached the *hacienda* from which he intended to depart, and where such a raft could be constructed, in mid-December. Starting his stay as a guest, he felt increasingly like a prisoner: whereas Evelyn Waugh's hero in *A Handful of Dust* had been compelled to stay in the Amazon jungle to read Dickens to his host, Snow was compelled to stay and play endless games of chess with his.

Eventually the craft was completed, but it was not until June that Snow managed to get away. And when he did, it was to be a short-lived episode, because the cataracts proved too intractable for the raft. Having had such a brief and frustrating experience after so long a wait, most people would have given up the idea of following the river altogether. But not so Snow. He again took to his feet, this time aided by mules and muleteers, until he came to another point near the Marañon

* *My Amazon Adventure* published by Odhams, London (undated).

[155]

where he could find a canoe and a canoer and ultimately set about the construction of yet another raft. He was still upstream of the normally accepted navigable point, and more rapids had to be negotiated—this time with the help of a more skilful paddler—before he eventually reached the more tranquil waters of Borja. From Borja it was relatively plain sailing to Iquitos, civilization, and a steamer to Manaus and Belém.

Snow had been travelling for nine months, after suffering —like Bates—from dysentery, sometimes limping from his broken thigh, always peering through the spray on his spectacles (there were only two sorts of white men known to the Indians in these parts—'pilots', without spectacles, and 'engineers', with spectacles), and peculiarly vulnerable to upsets of the rafts or canoes because he was a non-swimmer. He had opened a decade of Amazonian travel in which his schoolfellows were to play a disproportionate part.

Two or three years later, two undergraduates, one of them another Old Etonian, were sitting up late into the night in their rooms at Oxford scouring an atlas of the world for somewhere to perform a memorable journey. They recalled Sebastian Snow's *Adventure* on the Amazon and hit on the idea of doing a somewhat parallel journey—but in the opposite direction and by land. They would take a jeep across South America at its widest point, from Recife on the north-east Atlantic coast of Brazil to Lima on the Pacific coast of Peru. Although they would be travelling south of the Amazon itself, they would be far north of the only transcontinental road and would have to cross Mato Grosso and traverse many of the Amazon's main tributaries. They reasoned with each other that such a journey must be possible because Indian villages would never be more than 'two or three hundred miles apart' and there must be some track between villages. Both suppositions—as they were to discover—were erroneous.

The two undergraduates were Richard Mason and Robin Hanbury-Tenison. They eventually set out together in 1958 with no very clear idea of the route they were to take, but with a conviction that if they drove ever westwards by whatever tracks they could find, and if they enquired at each village or settlement the best way to get on to the next one, then—step by step—they would cross the continent as no other traveller before them had done. Pride apart, they could not afford to fail because the jeep in which they travelled had been *lent* to them by the manufacturers and there were heavy financial forfeits to be paid if it was not brought back.

Day after day they drove on; and night after night they slung their hammocks from a tree to the roof rack of the jeep and slept—relatively immune from insects and reptiles. On at least one occasion they found the spoor of a jaguar clearly traceable on the ground beneath their hammocks in the morning.

At Carolinus, a small town on the river Tocantins, the last existing road or track to the west came to an abrupt end at the river bank, and there was no ferry. They turned south, following rough paths and fording rivers, sometimes floating the jeep across on rafts, sometimes getting bogged down in swamps. They crossed the territory of the Xerente Indians, occasionally befriended by missionaries, and reached the banks of the Araguaya (Peter Fleming's river). At this point they had to build their own raft and, using two canoes as floats, paddled for five hours (across the lesser branch of the Araguaya) to the island of Bananal, which is formed by the two branches of the Araguaya. It is the largest inland island in the world but no vehicle had ever reached its banks before.

Here, in the heartland of the uncertain-tempered Karaja Indians, disaster struck. As the jeep lurched its way through the scrub country at the southern end of Bananal island, the chassis broke: it snapped clean through on both sides just behind the front wheels, depositing the engine on the ground. There was no question of being able to repair it without welding equipment, and no possibility of finding such equipment within a thousand kilometres of roadless, and often trackless country. Richard Mason and Robin Hanbury-Tenison tossed a coin—as good Englishmen should—to decide which of them would go off to seek help, and which of them would stay to guard the broken jeep and their equipment from the Karaja Indians. It fell to Hanbury-Tenison to go.

His lonely journey to Anapolis, partly on foot, partly on a borrowed horse (it was necessary to swim the rivers with the horse), partly by truck, was accomplished with remarkably little delay. The worse problem began at Anapolis where it was necessary to persuade a Greek garage owner to risk another jeep as well as his life (all urban dwellers in Brazil consider the *selva*—or forests—to be beset with lethal hazards and a land of no return) to go off with an unknown young Englishman to an unknown destination deep in the *selva* to mend an unknown vehicle with an unknown degree of damage. It was a considerable tribute to Hanbury-Tenison's powers of persuasion that he got the garage owner not only to set out, but to persist even after it became clear that the breakdown was far further away than Hanbury-Tenison had confessed and that the latter had lost his way on the return journey. But get back to Richard Mason and the broken vehicle he did after twelve days, and found that Mason had survived—leading a Robinson-Crusoe-like existence, fishing for piranha, shooting alligators and anaconda, being bitten by a stingray, cutting down trees and eating up his precious rations. The garage owner welded the crippled chassis together: the expedition was—if not on the road—at least on the track again.

Turning south-west again, the travellers entered the territory of the warrior Xavante tribe who two years earlier had murdered an Italian family of settlers in this area. They made friends with the Xavante and then pressed on further west, striking civilization for a moment at Cuiabá (the town from which Fawcett had set out) and narrowly escaping being shot when they inadvertently surprised an illicit *caxaça* factory in the bush. Skirting the north of the Pantanal swamps, they entered Bolivia and here, in the Banadoz of Izozog, they had to harness oxen to drag the battered jeep through the worst swamps they had yet encountered. But when they emerged it was to climb into the Andes and to complete their journey to the Pacific coast of Peru. They had done what no one before had done; they had driven across South America from east to west at its widest point; the Royal Geographical Society in London awarded them medals on their return. But neither of them had yet had a surfeit of Amazonian travel.

Richard Mason was to be the first back. During his crossing with Hanbury-Tenison he had always regretted that the jeep confined them to the line of least resistance; he wanted to go deeper into the jungle than any wheels could penetrate, and he wanted to get into the heart of that part of Mato Grosso which they had had to skirt around. Beyond Fleming's Araguaya lay Fawcett's Xingu, and beyond the Xingu lay an unknown and unexplored river, as remote in the 1960s as Roosevelt's Rio da Dúvida: this was the Iriri. Mason's plan was to lead a proper expedition, with Brazilian experts, guides and helpers, to discover the source of the Iriri and then to descend its length by canoe. His English companion on this was yet another Old Etonian—John Hemming, subsequently himself to become the director of the Royal Geographical Society, the author of *Red Gold* (quoted in earlier chapters) and one of the greatest living authorities on the Amazon.

In 1961, Mason and his companions were well established in Mato Grosso in the heart of the unknown area they wished to explore. Supplies had been brought up to a small airstrip called Posto Cachimbo and from there a trail had been blazed to a point on the Iriri river some thirty miles away; here the necessary canoes were being constructed for the exploratory voyage down-stream. There was a good deal of coming and going down the track, between the base and the river, by members of the expedition either carrying supplies or hunting for the pot. No trace of Indians, let alone hostile Indians, had been discovered. People felt so secure on the trail that they had begun to go alone. And this is what Richard Mason did.

One day as he passed through a clearing and disappeared into the darkness of the forest he was struck down from behind: he was shot through the body with eight arrows, his skull and his thigh broken by clubs. He almost certainly died instantly, probably unaware to the last of the ambush into which he had walked.

The most curious aspect of the murder—as with most murders—was who had killed him and why? At first his friends thought it might have been the Kayapo tribe, jealous of intrusion into their hunting areas. But when the clubs and arrows left behind at Mason's body were examined by other Indians they were unanimous in declaring that the distinctive binding of the arrows were those of the dreaded Kreen-Akrore —a tribe reputed to be of great stature and strength but never peaceably contacted by white men or other Indians: in fact, a totally unknown tribe of unusual ferocity. One theory among anthropologists was that the Kreen-Akrore might be descendants of Indians who had only escaped massacre and enslavement in the previous century by fleeing ever further into the most impenetrable fastness of the Amazon jungle, and who had maintained their understandable hostility to all *civilizados*.

The two greatest Brazilian authorities on the Amazonian Indians—the brothers Claudio and Orlando Villas-Boas (the latter of whom played a rôle recorded in an earlier chapter in connection with tracing the remains of Colonel Fawcett) —determined now to contact the Kreen-Akrore. It was to be the patient work of years. And they were accompanied in their task by a young Englishman, who had already made one adventurous trip to this part of the world, called Adrian Cowell.

Cowell's account* relates how he spent month after month getting closer to the elusive tribe, finding their trails, entering their deserted village, leaving presents to tempt them to come back, and always sensing that—while this activity was going on—the Kreen-Akrore were forever watching the intruders from the fringes of the jungle along the path, river bank or clearing. There were killings by the Kreen-Akrore and of the Kreen-Akrore, involving other tribes but not Europeans. Cowell's book and prize-winning television programme (he was accompanied by camera-men on most of his travels) convey the tension of the search: when eventually they nosed their canoes down the unknown Peixoto Azevedo river, on which the Kreen-Akrore had killed all previous intruders, they were keenly aware of their vulnerability while they handled the canoes down the rapids; part of the expedition moved down the river banks to give cover and protection to those exposed on or in the water.

On the face of it, it must have seemed that as the Villas-Boas brothers led Cowell down their river little had changed since Rondon had led Roosevelt down his river fifty years before. But the motive of the expedition had altered: no longer was hunting or even exploration its main purpose; now anthropology and a desire to protect the Indians from the ravages of outsiders and the internecine strife of tribal conflicts was the main motivation. Both Cowell and Hanbury-Tenison were to pursue these objectives further by their activities in England.

But pure adventure still played a part. In 1964 Sebastian Snow approached Robin Hanbury-Tenison with a wild idea: 'to bisect the South American continent from north to south by river'. He was convinced that the mouth of the Orinoco in Venezuela could be linked by water, through the Amazon river system, with the mouth of the River Plate 6,000 miles away in Argentina. The best way to prove it seemed to be to take an

* *The Tribe that Hides from Man* published by Bodley Head, London 1973.

[161]

inflatable rubber dinghy, with two powerful outboard motors, and try to travel down the Orinoco, the Casiquiare and the Rio Negro to Manaus, then down the Madeira and the Guaporé and then over the watershed to the Jaurú, the Paraguay and the Parana. In all this route there were only three places—one watershed and two sets of rapids—where any portage was necessary.

Although only part of this memorable journey was strictly in the Amazon Basin, it certainly forms a part of the story of Anglo-Saxon travel in the region. The first leg of the journey, linking the Orinoco and the Amazon, had been achieved at various times since Sir Thomas Roe had been the first Englishman to make the connection in 1610, as recounted in an earlier chapter. The most remarkable geographical feature of this section of the route was the Casiquiare, the river which runs out of the Orinoco over the watershed and into the Amazon basin. Once on the Rio Negro they had to shoot the rapids at São Gabriel de Cachoeira as Wallace, Spruce and Wickham had done before them. For Snow and Hanbury-Tenison, this leg was dominated by the former's ill health: migraines and loss of balance—a dangerous failing for a non-swimmer in a small boat—obliged him reluctantly to go first into hospital in Manaus and then to fly home. Hanbury-Tenison went on alone.

From Manaus he went down the Madeira river to Porto Velho and then, as generations of earlier travellers had found, the long series of rapids from San Antonio to Guajara Mirim on the Marmoré river required circumvention by the Madeira-Marmoré railway. Hanbury-Tenison loaded his frail craft on the train and then shared the footplate with a pistol-toting engine-driver, helping him stoke the furnace with logs as the train trundled through the forest like something out of Jules Vernes' *Round the World in Eighty Days*.

But it was the final stretch in the Amazon basin that was really the toughest part of the whole river journey. The

Marmoré river was followed for a hundred miles and then he turned up the Guaporé; here the *seringuiros* (rubber tappers) warned him that the Indians were dangerous on some of the stretches of river ahead; he was advised to go ashore on the jungle banks as seldom as possible and camp on islands whenever he could. Logs and weeds impeded the propellers. The open channel was often only a few feet wide as the river neared its source. Trees overhung the water and Hanbury-Tenison found that he was 'speeding through a dark tunnel of undergrowth'. It was with some relief that he reached the highest navigable point of the Guaporé and faced the portage over the watershed to the river systems of the Paraguay and Parana.

Villa Belo de Mato Grosso, the small settlement where he disembarked to look for transport, was a frontier town in the old tradition; a gun fight had just taken place in the main street; the loser had been buried and the winner first locked up in the sheriff's store and then allowed to escape to save everyone bother. It was characteristic of Hanbury-Tenison that he made friends with the sheriff and got hold of a truck to drive him and his boat through the forest to the upper reaches of the Jaurú and so on to the Paraguay river. He was to emerge at the River Plate in Buenos Aires to be hailed as 'El Intrepido'.

By the end of the same year—1965—another intrepid Englishman (also as it happens an Old Etonian) was spending four months on the Amazon researching a book about the history and wildlife of the river: Robin Furneaux* travelled down the Araguaya and the Kuluene, in the heart of the Fawcett country, and made a memorable journey from Manaus to Iquitos under the auspices of a charlatan and crook

---

* Later to become the 3rd Earl of Birkenhead and to die tragically early, in 1985, having given the present author much generous help in the preparation of this book. His own book, entitled *The Amazon: the Story of a Great River* was published by Hamish Hamilton in 1969 and is still an invaluable work for all interested in the river.

whose propensity for generating intrigue and misinformation rivalled that attributed by Peter Fleming to the appalling Major Pingle of *Brazilian Adventure*.

There is a famous chapter in St Paul's Epistle to the Hebrews which reads in part:

> 'And what more should I say? For the time would fail me to talk of Gideon and of Barak . . . who . . . subdued kingdoms, wrought righteousness, obtained promises, stopped the mouths of lions, quenched the violence of fire, escaped the edge of the sword, waxed valiant . . . they wandered in dens and caves of the earth.'

The chronicler of the achievements of contemporary Anglo-Saxon adventurers on the Amazon has the same problem as that encountered by St Paul in his splendid chronicle of the achievements of those professing true faith: however memorable and worthy they are just too many to be recounted without overtaxing the patience and attention of the reader. The time would fail me to tell of Francis Huxley and of Peter Matthieson, of Nicholas Guppy and of Gordon MacCreagh, of Gilbert Phelps and David Maybury Lewis, of Matthew Huxley and Cornell Capa, of Anthony Smith and many others, who —even if they did not subdue kingdoms and stop the mouths of lions—at least discovered tribes, obtained promises, and occasionally stopped the mouths of jaguars and alligators. The tradition of trespassing on the Amazon has not died.

EPILOGUE

I wrote in the Prologue to this book that I had tried to see for myself the conditions which my compatriots and other Anglo-Saxon travellers had encountered. This has involved much travelling, not only by light aircraft and by road, but also on foot and by canoe. From time to time some character and some set of circumstances have fixed themselves in my mind as a continuing part of the story.

The spirit of Bates and Wallace lives on in Amazonas today in various incarnations. A young Englishman, employed by the National Institute for Amazonian Research, camps alone in a region of primary jungle to the north of Manaus in order to study the behaviour patterns of primates; he watches his monkeys day after day and week after week until he can recognize every member of every family. His study is not an idle one as he has a very specific set of questions always in the front of his mind: how much territory does a monkey require to bring up its family and carry on a 'normal' life? How many hectares or square kilometres does each different species require? The answer—when he determines it—will help decide what can be the smallest viable area of forest worth preserving from this point of view (others are studying the life patterns of other fauna) when new roads and clearances dissect and diminish existing tracts of primary jungle. Meanwhile, the Englishman goes about his daily business much as Bates did when he set out on his daily routine from Belém, with his insect box, his game bag, his thongs on which to hang lizards and his lepidopterist's pincushion.

Further up-river, a lone Englishwoman is to be encountered

travelling by canoe with two Indian paddlers. Over the past several decades Margaret Mee might have been observed on almost any tributary of the Amazon. Her canoe has curious impedimenta loaded into it: an easel, paint boxes, folios of stiff cartridge paper. She is less interested than her compatriot down-stream in the fauna around her—almost, in fact, oblivious to its possible menace. For her the flora of the Amazon forest is the lure to these regions of green light and vivid orchids, of dark undergrowth and exuberant foliage. Meticulously she studies and reproduces the colours and shapes of the forest flowers. Like Lizzie Hessel, the Victorian lady who travelled so widely on the Rio Negro, it does not occur to her that she is doing anything odd, let alone brave. She is wholly absorbed—like Richard Spruce—in the novelty and splendour of the plant life around her. When her quiet voyage is over, she will return to her studio in Rio de Janeiro to work on her sketches.

Further south, in the new state of Rondônia (named after Colonel—finally Marshal—Rondon) and near the banks of the Roosevelt river, the forest is already encroached upon by farmers and developers. This is no longer explorers' territory but a new-frontier land where—as in the North-American West in the last century—conflicts arise between indigenous Indians and new settlers, between *garimpeiros* (individual prospectors and miners—usually for gold) and large mining companies, between established land-owners and squatters. It is a region where government and central authority—however resolute—can seem a long way away, where private retribution may seem swifter and easier to come by than the due processes of law. Such fluid societies attract exploiters, but they also attract champions of those who are perceived to be the losers —be they Indians or landless tenant farmers. Father Luke is one of these self-appointed champions. A tall fair-skinned American evangelist, he walks alone through regions which few other parish priests or even missionaries reach, giving advice and practical help as he sees it to those who seem the weakest in this rough and tough society. To some he appears an agitator, to others a saint. To himself, he is a lineal descendant of Walt Hardenburg and Roger Casement.

Far to the west of Rondônia in the Cordillera Blanca of Peru, near the very source of the Marañon river (the principal component of the Amazon—as it is to become) a bearded, broad-shouldered figure strides towards the skyline. He has come a long way from his native peaks of Derbyshire in England in order to be here. On his back is a massive pack. Hanging from his belt is a prismatic compass. He stops from time to time to take bearings and to consult a sketch map, encased in cellophane as a protection from the wind and showers. Black pots of curious shape and mysterious provenance have been discovered near here; some date from the pre-Inca civilization of Chavin—a ruin and village lying in the steep and sinister valley to the landward side of the cordillera; some seem to defy attribution and to hail from an as-yet-undiscovered archaeological site. The youthful figure with the pack is pursuing his own hunt for stones which may reveal their secrets. Like Colonel Fawcett or Evelyn Waugh's Tony Last, he is in search of a city.

Other figures too, some of them all too fleetingly encountered, intensify the impression of continuity among the trespassers. There was the road engineer from Ohio working with his theodolite as a consultant on a troublesome section of the Transamazonica highway, who reminded one of Colonel Church or Neville Craig on their rugged surveys along the Madeira and Mamoré rivers.

There was the dubious character from Florida slipping across the unpatrolled frontier where the Brazilian township of Tabatinga trails its dusty road into the Colombian township of Leticia—at a bend in the Amazon where it changes its Brazilian name of Solimões for its Peruvian name of Marañon —with a load of contraband that seemed likely to be much more dangerous and illicit than Wickham's purloined rubber seeds.

There was the master of the Booth Line* cargo vessel whom we encountered on the quay-side at Belém—as we embarked for a visit to a buffalo ranch on the island of Marajó in the mouth of the Amazon—who knew the river as intimately as that Captain Murray who had put his ship at the disposal of Wickham. He quoted to us some of the timeless nautical statistics of the Amazon: how at its mouth the two banks are further apart than London and Paris; how one fifth of all the world's fresh water flows down its river system, and how even a hundred miles out from its estuary—such is the force of the fresh water emerging—a sailor can draw drinking water from the ocean.

There was the hunter from the Appalachian Mountains whom we stumbled on while innocently fishing in the Pantanal —the swamps of southern Mato Grosso—who seemed not to have heard that alligators were now protected and who blazed away with as much zest as Teddy Roosevelt or Peter Fleming. All these seemed to be direct descendants of characters whom I had come to know as part of the history of my compatriots in these parts.

But my abiding and haunting impression is none of these, but of one who—perhaps uniquely—seemed to have broken away from the invariable role of trespasser played by Anglo-Saxons on the Amazon, who seemed almost to be accepted as belonging there, who certainly 'wrought righteousness' and 'waxed valiant' as surely as any in the long roll of honour quoted in the last chapter.

During our stay at the Silesian mission station at Para-cachoeira on the Rio Uaupés (near where this tributary of the

* The Booth Line have been sending ships up the Amazon since 1866 when Charles Booth sailed from Liverpool on the maiden voyage of the *Augustine*. Many must have been their adventures, but unhappily the records of the company were largely destroyed during the blitz in the Second World War.

Rio Negro crosses the border from Colombia to Brazil) we had heard so much of Sister Betsy from California that we were sad at having missed her. It was she who had 'adopted' a Tucano Indian orphan child at the mission school: a child who, when the other children were collected by their fathers for the long river journey home to their villages at the end of term (often five or six days by canoe), had nowhere to go until Sister Betsy took her under her wing. It was she who raised so much money for the mission by her lectures in her home state. It was she who was sent for by distant Tucano villagers when there was sickness or trouble in their homes. But we had had to leave Paracachoeira for our long-planned canoe trip up the *igarapes* —the forest branches closing over their dark waters—before the Sister returned to the mission. Our thoughts were elsewhere as we travelled silently into an overgrown world of foliage, not unlike Marvell's concept of a garden

'Annihilating all that's made
To a green thought in a green shade.'

So when we saw the upright, lone figure in the approaching dug-out canoe, as we rounded a bend in our stream, we did not guess immediately who it was. The gentle, rhythmic paddle strokes suggested long familiarity with these waters; the loose white robe with its head-covering seemed a practical protection against the sun and insects, rather than the conventional uniform of a convent. But Sister Betsy it was.

She greeted us as if our appearance—300 miles from the nearest town and in the middle of the world's deepest jungle —was a pleasant but altogether natural occurrence: we might have been neighbours who had ridden over from the next-door ranch in California, or old acquaintances unexpectedly encountered in the supermarket.

'It's rather warm today, isn't it', she said, for all the world as if she were contemplating retreating to the marquee at a garden fête. It *was* rather warm, we agreed, as we wiped the sweat from our eyes, acutely conscious of the thermometer plunging upwards into the nineties fahrenheit.

Sister Betsy looked over her shoulder into the well of the canoe at an object hidden from our view.

'I wish I could stop for a chat', she said, 'but I don't think it would be fair on my passenger: he's really in rather a hurry'.

Passenger? Could the object in the well of the canoe be a child? We pulled along side and peered in. A full-grown man—an Indian covered in a blanket—lay faintly groaning in the half shade.

'It's really too late already', she said, as if apologizing. 'His leg's a goner and he may be too. They didn't kill the snake, so I'm not quite sure what it was. They always try their own medicines first. But then, why not: it's what they believe in. All the same . . .', and her words faltered a little, 'if only they'd paddled him down to the mission five days ago when it happened, we could have given him the serum and he'd have been walking by now. As it is we'll have to get him flown to São Gabriel or Manaus and they'll have to cut that leg off. No, I shouldn't look; it's not very pretty.'

We murmured inadequately. Could we help? No, she was nearly there. Could we transfer him to our larger canoe? No, it was probably best to move him as little as possible. She paddled on.

'Good luck!' we called after her.

She turned her head as she was almost disappearing round the next bend:

'Luck? It's not your good luck wishes I need—it's your prayers.' It was not a rebuke: it was a request.

It was the last we saw of her. As she disappeared the silence was total. But I think somewhere, on some ultimate river, the trumpets sounded for her.

SELECT BIBLIOGRAPHY

The principal published sources I have used are listed below.

ABREU, CAPISTRANO DE *O descubrimento do Brasil* (Rio de Janeiro 1929)

ACUÑA, CRISTÓBAL DE *Nuevo Descubrimiento del Gran Rio de las Amazonas* (Madrid 1641)

BATES, HENRY WALTER *The Naturalist on the River Amazons* (London 1892)

CAUFIELD, CATHERINE *In the Rainforest* (London 1985)

CHERRIE, GEORGE K. *Dark Trails: Adventures of a Naturalist* (New York 1930)

COLLIER, RICHARD *The River that God Forgot* (London 1968)

COWELL, ADRIAN *The Tribe that Hides from Man* (London 1973)

CRAIG, NEVILLE B. *Recollections of an ill fated expedition* (Philadelphia 1907)

DYOTT, G. M. *Man hunting in the jungle* (New York 1930)

EDWARDS, WILLIAM H. *A Voyage up the River Amazon* (London 1847)

FAWCETT, BRIAN *Ruins in the Sky* (London 1958)

FAWCETT, P. H. *Exploration Fawcett* (London 1953)

FLEMING, PETER *Brazilian Adventure* (London 1933)

FREYRE, GILBERTO *Ingleses no Brasil* (Rio de Janeiro 1948)

FURNEAUX, ROBIN *The Amazon* (London 1969)

FUSSELL, PAUL *Abroad* (New York 1980)

GELDERMAN, CAROL *Henry Ford: the Wayward Capitalist* (New York 1981)

HAKLUYT, RICHARD *The Principall Navigations, Voyages, Traffiques and Discoveries of the English Nation* (London 1589)

HANBURY-TENISON ROBIN *The Rough and the Smooth* (London 1969) *Worlds Apart* (London 1984)

HARDENBURG, W. E. *The Devil's Paradise* (London 1912)

HART-DAVIES, DUFF *Peter Fleming* (London 1974)

HEMMING, JOHN *Red Gold* (London 1978)

HOUSE OF COMMONS *Report and Special Report from the Select Committee on Putamayo, together with the proceedings of the Committee, minutes of evidence and appendices* (London 1913)

HUXLEY, FRANCIS *Affable Savages* (London 1956)

KINKEAD, GWEN *Article on 'Trouble in D. K. Ludwig's Jungle' in Fortune* (New York 1983)

LEONARDOS, OTHON HENRY *Geociências no Brasil: a contribuição britânica* (Rio de Janeiro 1970)

LEWIS, DAVID L. *The Public Image of Henry Ford* (Detroit 1976)

MaCCOLL, RENE *Roger Casement* (London 1937)

McINTYRE, LOREN *Article on Jari in National Geographic Magazine* (New York 1980)

MAW, HENRY LISTER, R. N. *Journal of a Passage from the Pacific to the Atlantic, crossing the Andes in the Northern Provinces of Peru and descending the River Marañon or Amazon* (London 1829)

MILLER, LEO E. *In the Wilds of South America* (New York 1919)

MORRISON, TONY (editor) *Lizzie: A Victorian lady's Amazon adventure* (London 1985)

MURPHY, TOM *Article on Fordlandia in Latin American Daily Post* (Rio de Janeiro 1983)

PURCHAS, SAMUEL *Hakluytus Postumus, or Purchas His Pilgrimes* (London 1625)

RALEIGH, SIR WALTER *The Discoverie of the large and bewtiful Empire of Guiana* (London 1596)

RONDON, C. M. DA SILVA *Lectures delivered at the Phenix Theatre of Rio de Janeiro in October 1915 on the Roosevelt-Rondon Scientific Expedition* (Rio de Janeiro 1916)

ROOSEVELT, THEODORE *Through the Brazilian Wilderness* (London 1914)

SMYTH, Lieut W., R.N. AND LOWE, Mr F., R.N. *Narrative of a journey from Lima to Pará* (London 1836)

SNOW, SEBASTIAN *My Amazon Adventure* (London, undated, but approx 1954)

SPRUCE, RICHARD *Notes of a Botanist on the Amazon and Andes* edited by A. R. Wallace (London 1908)

TOMLINSON, H. M. *The Sea and the Jungle* (London 1912)

TREVELYAN, G. M. *Grey of Fallodon* (London 1937)

VON HAGEN, VICTOR W. *South America Called Them* (London 1949)

WALLACE, A. R. *Narrative of Travels on the Amazon and Rio Negro* (London 1853)

WAUGH, EVELYN *Ninety-two Days* (London 1933)

WHIFFEN, Captain T. *The North West Amazonas* (London 1915)

WICKHAM, HENRY ALEXANDER *Rough Notes of a Journey Through the Wilderness, from Trinidad to Pará Brazil, by way of the Great Cataracts of the Orinoco, Atabapo and Rio Negro* (London 1872); *On the plantation, cultivation, and curing the Pará Indian rubber, with an account of its introduction from the West to the Eastern Tropics* (London 1908)

WILLIAMSON, JAMES A. *English Colonies in Guiana and on the Amazon 1604–68* (Oxford 1923)

INDEX

Abbott, Arthur, 122–3
Acre, Territory of, 67
Adriaansz, 24
alligators, 44–5, 136
Aloique, 117–18
Amazon Basin map, 21
Amazon Company, 24, 27
Amazonas, S.S., 51–2, 55
anaconda, 43–4
Anapolis, 158
Anti-Slavery Society, 76–7
Araguaya river, 130–31, 157
Arana, Julio Cesar, 70–2, 74–5, 78–80, 88–9
Aripuanan, 103

Bakairi, 114, 116
Bananal island, 157
Bates, Henry Walter, 33–47
Beare, Col., 109
Belém do Pará, 19, 22, 29, 37, 132
Belterra, 145–6
Bernardino, 116–17
Bertie, Col. Hon. Reginald, 80, 82
Betsy, Sister, 169–70
Bingham, Hiram, 111
boa-constrictors, 44
Booth Line ships, 168

Casement, Sir Roger, 72, 80–85
Cherrie, George, 92, 93, 101, 104, 106
Church, Col. George Earl, 58–60, 63
Cockeram, Martin, 15–16
Collins, P. & T. (contractors), 60–63
Collins, Tom, 61–2
Condamine, Charles de la, 30
Cowell, Adrian, 160–61
Craig, Neville, 62, 64
Cuna, Muchu, 25

de Orellana, Francisco, 26

Dead Horse Camp, 115
Digby, Lord, 22
Dyott, Commander George, 116, 124

Edwards, William H., 32–3
El Dorado, 108
El Encanto, 72–3

Farquhar, Percival, 68
Fawcett, Brian, 117, 120–24
Fawcett, Jack, 114, 126
Fawcett, Col. Percy, 107–27
Felipe, 112
Fitzcarrald, Carlos, 66
Fitzcarrald, Isthmus of, 66
Fleming, Peter, 128–39
Ford, Henry, 143–7
Fordlandia, 144–5, 147
Fry, Capt. Roger, 28
Furneaux, Robin, 163

Gibbon, Lt. Lardner, 58
Gielgud, Henry, 80, 82–3, 86–7
Gondomar, Count, 20, 22, 24
Goodwin, Consul General, 125
Grey, Sir Edward, 72, 80, 85
Gubbins, John Russell, 75, 79, 87, 89
Guiana Company, 27, 28

Hanbury-Tenison, Robin, 156–9, 161–3
Hardenburg, Walt, 69–79, 88
Harris, Rev. John, 76–7
Hawkins, Sir William, 15–16
Heath, Edwin, 65
Hemming, John, 27, 159
Hessel, Fred, 65–6
hevea brasiliensis (rubber plant), 50
Hixson, Thomas, 28
Holman, Capt. J. G., 129–38
Hooker, Dr. Joseph, 50, 55

Iquitos, 73
Iriri river, 159

Jaguars, 43, 140/146
Jari river, 150, 151
Jesuit missionaries, 30
Julio, 101–102

Kalapolo Indians, 117–21
Karaja Indians, 157, 158
Knivet, Anthony, 16–17
Kreen-Akrore tribe, 160–61
Kuliseu river, 118
Kuluene river, 118

Lister-Kaye, Sir John, 76, 79, 88, 89
Lowe, Lt., 31
Ludwig, Daniel K., 147–53

Madeira, River, 57
Madeira/Mamoré railway, 59, 63, 162
Marañon, 155
Markham, Clements, 49, 55
Mason, Richard, 156–60
Mathys, Lizzie, 65–6
Maw, Henry, 31
Mee, Margaret, 166
melina trees, 148
Moennich, Martha, 126
Monte Dourado, 150
Murray, Capt., 51–2, 55
Murray, John (publisher), 31, 32

North, Capt. Roger, 20, 22–4

O'Brien, Bernard, 25–7
Orellana, Francisco de, 26, 154
Orinoco, River, 17, 161–2
Orton, James, 64–5

Paget, Sir Ralph, 123, 124
Panama Canal, 67, 68
Paracachoeira, 168
Paternoster, Sydney, 77
Perkins, W. B., 69–74
Peruvian Amazon Company, 70–89
Petropolis, Treaty of, 67
power-plant project, 150–51
pulp-mill project, 150–51
Purcell, Philip, 26

Putamayo, River, 69–71

Quinine, 49

Railway scheme, Madeira/Mamoré,
    58–64, 67–8
Raleigh, Sir Walter, 17–18
Rattin, Stefano, 121–7
Read, Henry, 76, 79, 89
Reilly, 'Butch', 112
Rimmell, Raleigh, 114, 126
Rio Castanho, 103
Rio da Dúvida, 92–3
Rio Roosevelt, 98, 103
Roe, Sir Thomas, 18–19
Rondon, Col., 92–106, 111
Rondônia, 166
Roosevelt, Kermit, 92, 93–4, 96, 99, 101
Roosevelt, Theodore, 91–106
rubber, 49–56, 143–6

Santarém, 49, 50
Serrano, David, 71
Simplicio, 96
Smyth, Lt., 31
Snow, Sebastian, 154–6, 161–2
Spruce, Richard, 33–47, 166

Tapajós river, 144, 145
Tapirapé, 130–31, 135, 136
Teixeira, Pedro, 27–8
tobacco, 23
Tordesillas, treaty of, 29

Villa Belo de Mato Grosso, 163
Villas-Boas, Claudio, 160–61
Villas-Boas, Orlando, 119–21,
    160–61
von Humboldt, Baron, 31

Wallace, Alfred Russel, 33–47
Waterton, Charles, 31
Waugh, Evelyn, 139–42
Whiffen, Capt., 79–80, 88
White, William, 23
Wickham, Henry Alexander, 48–55
wood pulp project, 148–52

Xavante tribe, 158
Xingu River, 24, 118